Musing
in search of
Meaning

Musing
in search of
Meaning

Randall Mishoe

Musing in search of Meaning

Library of Congress Control Number: 2021912449

ISBN: 978-1-7361072-0-1

ACKNOWLEDGMENTS

Having lived this long, the friends, teachers, groups, and institutions that shaped my life and the thought in this book are too numerous to list. Some have long since passed over the horizon of this world and gone to their reward. I regret not naming them as well as so many of you who remain in the orbit of our shared existence. So it is that my acknowledgment will focus on the more immediate group of persons who in ways great and small gave inspiration to the words that found their way to these pages.

In brief, I acknowledge:

- The Department of Psychology and Clinical Studies at Andover Newton Theological School and the faculty members who shaped a contemporary understanding of Curia Animarum, the Care of Souls. Those faculty members include John Billinsky, Henry Brooks, and Paul Huss.
- Barbara and Lee, who joined me in my Odyssey to New England and made the winters less frigid.
- The ongoing members of our Dream Group of some 30 years—Ann, Beverly, Bud, Dusty, Lynn, and Michael—who bore the themes of life and death with grace, humor, insight, and transformative humanity.

~ Deborah, who wore many hats: editor, critic, encourager, humorist, scriptural concordance, and existential philosopher.

~ My publishing team: Richard Griffin, consultant; Kathy Brown, editor; Kim Hall, design.

~ The analysands who opened their hearts and minds in our sessions, teaching me deeper levels of courage and honesty.

~ Devlin Cyr Wallace, cover design.

The mandala is a montage of geological formations and ancient rock art residing within the labyrinthic landscapes of West Virginian cave systems. These include speleogens, rimstone, flowstone, stalagmites, stalactites, and anastomosis. The central image is of an ancient Native American petroglyph and a marker for those who seek to journey into the depths.

To my wife,
Deborah,
whose love moved mountains

CONTENTS

CHAPTER FOUR:
THE ULTIMATE QUESTION 139

GLOSSARY 181

NOTES AND REFERENCES 187

PERMISSIONS 191

INDEX 193

ABOUT THE AUTHOR 195

INTRODUCTION

I n the pages that follow, you will find a number of topics
having to do with interdisciplinary reflections in matters
of:

soul and body
nature and spirit
sickness and health
creativity and destruction
stagnation and growth
religion and secularism
death and life
community and solitariness
conformity and individuality
suffering and healing

I hope my musings will be of interest to individuals in
all walks of life. They are intended for each of us who looks
for some meaningful way to consider the affairs of life from
a depth perspective.

And for those who desire, the musings may become a
ritual to be shared in the spirit of William Stafford's reflective
poem that I leave with you:

A RITUAL TO READ TO EACH OTHER

If you don't know the kind of person I am
and I don't know the kind of person you are
a pattern that others made may prevail in the world
and following the wrong God home, we may miss
our star.

For there is many a small betrayal in the mind,
a shrug that lets the fragile sequence break
sending with shouts the horrible errors of childhood
storming out to play through the broken dike.

And as elephants parade holding each elephant's
tail, but if one wanders, the circus won't find the
park, I call it cruel and maybe the root of all cruelty
to know what occurs but did not recognize the fact.

And so I appeal to a voice to something shadowy,
a remote important region in all who talk:
though we could fool each other, we should
consider—lest the parade of our mutual life get lost
in the dark.

For it is important that awake people be awake,
or a breaking line may discourage them back to
sleep; the signals we give—yes or no, or maybe—
should be clear: the darkness around us is deep.

CHAPTER ONE

DREAMS

*The dream is the small hidden door in the deepest
and most intimate sanctum of the soul.*
—*C. G. Jung*

THE STORY OF YOUR LIFE
FROM INSIDE OUT

At the end, how shall we describe our lives? The usual way, of course, is to think of them much like we write our résumés: a short section dealing with our personal history, another part focusing on education, a much longer section listing work accomplishments (hopefully) and recognitions, and finally, some remarks about our place in the family and community.

But that way of telling our life stories, while helpful in marking our places within the collective life of society, does not really describe the living drama within our souls: those roads not taken, the grief or guilt or despair about choices made and not made, and the moments of bravery or cowardice when we acted unfaithfully toward others and perhaps ourselves. Or if we by chance did indeed confess those interior moments, very few of us describe the images that motivated us and the mythic beliefs that fascinated and perhaps even terrorized us.

I am not suggesting that we must "tell all" to the public. However, I am advocating on behalf of becoming conscious of this interiority. I am saying I think it can be beneficial to tell our stories from the "inside out," at least to ourselves. What we then do with the stories can be decided only once we have a greater consciousness of what they are.

Why bother to do this? Why not let the "sleeping dogs" lie quietly within our psyches? I believe the telling of our life stories from the inside out makes possible a fuller, more meaningful embrace of ourselves. Life seems to appreciate closures as much as beginnings. Such closure brings peace and the grace of acceptance, but it also quite surprisingly uncovers some occasional nuggets of treasure like long-forgotten family heirlooms lost in the attics and basements of our mental lives.

So how do we begin to tell the story of our lives from the inside out? In his essay titled "The Symbolic Life," Carl Jung puts it this way:

> *So these depths, that layer of utter unconscious-*
> *ness in our dream, contain at the same time the*
> *key to individual completeness and wholeness, in*
> *other words to healing. The meaning of 'whole' or*
> *'wholeness' is to make holy or to heal. The descent*
> *into the depths will bring healing. It is the way*
> *to the total being, to the treasure which suffering*
> *mankind is forever seeking, which is hidden in the*

*place guarded by terrible danger. This is the place
of primordial unconsciousness and at the same time
the place of healing and redemption, because it
contains the jewel of wholeness. It is the cave where
the dragon of chaos lives and it is also the indestruc-
tible city, the magic circle or temenos, the sacred
precinct where all the split-off parts of the personality are united. (CW 18, para. 270)*

In other words, our dreams tell the story of our lives
from a vantage point we seldom think about. Unless we are
shaken by a very disturbing nightmare, we most often can
throw off our dreams as so much baggage, trash, or refuse
that we don't really need and would be better off without. At
least, we could sleep better without them, so we think. But
the fact is that our dreams are vital with their subtle, quiet,
and sometimes insistent nagging to get our attention and—
perhaps—to redirect a course of action or make possible
some important change in our attitude or state of mind.

Consider, for example, these five basic questions of life,
to which I will return later:

1. **Who am I?** This is the question of IDENTITY.
    If you sit down to think about it, the answer is a
    rather complicated one that takes you far beyond
    your job, marital status, and titles.

2. **Where do I belong?** The question of COMMUNITY. Again, not so easy to answer if you really think about it, this question prompts you to consider who your true friends are, what group you really identify with most if you are honest with yourself, and any pretensions or obsessions about clubs you belong to or wish you could.

3. **Where am I to go?** The question of VOCATION. The question, in this sense, looks at vocation as a calling. In other words, from "outside" myself something or someone "calls" to me, gets my attention, and resonates with some deep-seated longing to fulfill myself.

4. **What should I do?** The question of ETHICS. A healthy psychological life is one that is moral, and by that I do not mean moralistic. The deep story of humanity's most profound heroism is the story of seeking a moral ground. It is the message that Shakespeare put in the mouth of Polonius as advice to his son Laertes who was leaving to go into the wider unknown and morally uncertain world: "To thine own self be true, and then it must follow as night follows day, thou canst be false to no one" (*Hamlet,* 1.3.84).

5.   **Why?** The question of our SPIRITUALITY.

> "Tell me why the stars do shine?
> Tell me why the ivy twine?
> Tell me why the skies are blue?
> And I will tell you just why I love you."

So goes the lovely old folk tune. But it sounds the archetypal theme within each of us who has marveled at the mystery of creation and felt we belonged to something much bigger and meaningful than can be either explained or cast in doctrinal formulas.

These are the existential questions of our life: Identity, Community, Vocation, Ethics, and Spirituality. Told from the inside out, they portray the mythopoeic dramas by which each life is granted its own place in the starry heavens. And, if we look back closely, we will likely be surprised at the many times our dreams have nudged us in one way or another when we wrestled with each of the questions. These dreams make up a library of countless dramas with casts of thousands.

Each dream is that important, that deserving of our attention and at least a recall of the night's adventure. And for people who are interested in taking a closer look at their lives from the inside out, here is a possible approach for gathering, listening to, learning from, and aligning themselves with a story within that wants to be lived out.

Dreams come to us each night. Our response is:

1. To remember.

2. To record.

3. To reflect.
   a. Note the "story" the dream tells.
   b. Be attentive to the setting, the characters, and the actions of the characters as well as our own behavior.
   c. Identify the psychological complex the dream may be surfacing.
   d. Consider whether the dream is subjective (the imagery's focus is to identify inner parts of myself) or objective (the imagery's focus is directed toward persons and/or events outside myself).
   e. Note how the dream is likely compensating for imbalance in our waking life, unless the dream is telepathic, precognitive, or focusing on past trauma.
   f. Connect the dream with past dreams.
   g. Observe the imagery's themes that may have appeared in myths, fairy tales, movies, or books.

    h. Consider the larger context of the past day's
       activities, events in our wider culture and
       world, and the spiritual or religious themes we
       may be facing.
    i. State an interpretation and notice how it feels.

4. To re-envision.

Imagine how your life will be different as you live into the dream's imagery. How will you act, think, feel, perceive? What difference might this make in your basic attitude and outlook in life? Does this lead you toward greater health, completeness, or fulfillment? If you are uncertain, discuss the prospects with a reliable person.

5. To redirect.

This is the point where you are given opportunities to make changes in your behavior and possibly in your lifestyle. You may gain a sense of fulfillment that you have not realized before. This is the point where a new world begins.

In conclusion, the truth is that we live our lives as a succession of many worlds, with beginnings, middles, and ends. Only at the end might we really see how these worlds make one life. But the meaning of this one life can only be most fully appreciated when we tell the story from inside out.

DREAMS AND JUNGIAN DREAMWORK

D reams come to each of us, and ways of working with dreams may be found in countless books and offerings on the web. I salute all of you who, like me, follow your dreams and dreamwork with a passion.

You may wonder, however, how dreamwork takes place in analysis. Is it different from simply working with dreams on your own? My answer is yes and no. When we come into the process of analysis, we generally commit ourselves to the work of examining our personalities in depth. That in itself influences the kind of dreams that may come, you see? In other words, the psyche responds to the work at hand. And if there is a specific focus of Jungian analysis, we will be led through the portals that enable us to journey with some intentionality toward "individuation," and from a perspective that is synthetic, prospective, and teleological.

Consider these three words: *synthetic* (uniting the opposites that are unresolved in our lives), *prospective* (considering the potential that lies hidden within the unconscious), and *teleological* (pointing toward an "end" that represents a culmination of one's life in its physical, mental, emotional, social, and spiritual dimensions). This Jungian perspective that is synthetic, prospective, and teleological emerges from a study of the human personality that reveals its purposiveness and creativity prompted by the unconscious that appears to nudge us with a kind of goal-directedness. Analysis thus becomes a "waking up" to the process within that is striving toward an actualization of our wholeness, the telos of which Jung chose the word *individuation*, to be distinguished from individualism and individuality—terms that catch the nuances of ego-directed activity and identity.

A person may thus be very charming, intellectual, nice, kind, cooperative, likable, religious, and accomplished in some facet of life, but still not "be awake." Jung compared the path toward individuation as having similar demands upon the human personality as the process of becoming a Zen adept under the tutelage of a Zen master. Jung says this:

> ... *let a Master set us to a hard task, which requires more than mere parrot-talk, and the European begins to have doubts, for the steep path of self-development is to him as mournful and gloomy as the path to hell. (CW 11, para. 902)*

Or, as Jesus of Nazareth is reported to have said in the Gospel of Luke when he was questioned about wealth and the Kingdom of God:

How hard it is for those who have riches to make
their way into the kingdom of God. Yes, it is easier
for a camel to pass through the eye of a needle than
for someone rich to enter the kingdom of God.
(Luke 18:24–27, RSV)

Obviously, Jesus is not just picking on the wealthy in this saying that appears in all the Synoptic Gospels and has reliability and authenticity. Like Jung describing each of us who shies away from the work when it gets hard, Jesus is saying there is something in human nature that can be intimidated by fear, uncertainty, and the challenge of great effort when it involves risk. However, like the child who fears taking that very first step or that very first time of taking the training wheels off the bicycle, we will continue to face the risk of all new steps until the day we die.

But individuation is a new kind of risk, not just an exercise in bravery. Bravery is not really the quality that we most need, although courage is important on our journey. Even more important is a trust and commitment to follow our star that guides us on the night-sea journey toward wholeness or individuation. And in our dreams, we find our star.

DREAMS, TIME, AND
RELIGIOUS EXPERIENCE

I often find myself with no words when individuals visit my consulting room, bringing concerns and questions of deep perplexity. At such a time, it is not a matter of intelligence or training or desire to understand the presenting dilemma. Rather, it is a need for patience and—most importantly— the expectation that something or someone will come. Not infrequently, a dream will be remembered with a cast of characters involved in a drama we could never make up. The dream may be long or short, but in any case, another presence makes itself known in the consulting room.

So it was when "Gita" appeared in a one-sentence dream. But first, some background.

The dreamer was a professional woman in her sixties. Accomplished, successful in her work, a practicing Protestant, a wife, and a mother, she was also a person haunted by a bothersome anxiety that something bad may happen to disrupt her strong efforts at organizing and making her life happy. The dreamer was very committed to her religious faith in a rather progressive denomination, and her shadow-like anxiety conflicted with her belief in a God who would protect her and vigilantly maintain a just world, safeguarding especially those persons seeking to live by the moral code she saw presented in the Bible.

With this as a brief background to my dreamer's life, and with her kind permission, I will share two quite evocative dreams she brought to our work. This was the first dream:

> *Two girls, around the age of seven or eight, are*
> *touring a house, talking and playing with each*
> *other. They go into a room—a kitchen?—and see*
> *on a shelf a small box. In the box is a snake moving*
> *around. I look it in the eye. Glancing around, I*
> *see a second snake on the counter. The first snake*
> *continues to look at me and me at him.*

When I asked my dreamer for her associations to the house, the young girls, and especially the snakes, she responded with a somewhat blasé air, revealing little affect, curiosity, or concern for the young girls or herself (who alternately experiences herself as observer and participant in the dream). Aware of my own heightened sense of danger, I asked her how she felt, particularly when she saw the snake and especially when she made eye contact and realized the first snake continued to hold her in its gaze. But she again appeared to slough off my questions and seemed to be impervious to any recognition of danger.

Allowing myself to sit for just a little while but holding in mind what seemed to me to be a response incongruent with the dreamer's description of her situation in the dream, I asked her if she thought her attitude and associations might be "Pollyanna."

She, in turn, and to her credit, held my question for a few seconds and—finally showing some emotion—said, "Yes, they might well be."

"Do you think you might approach other threatening situations in life with such an attitude?" I asked.

Then, in what appeared to be one of those moments when you come upon something deep and disturbing, she acknowledged that may be the case, that she felt uncomfortable facing threatening situations and would rather not dwell on them.

When she returned for her next appointment, the dreamer confessed to having a hard time giving up her Pollyanna attitude, a word she was now using to describe herself. Referring back to her theology, she said she found it hard to think of a God who left Jesus to suffer on a cross. That same God would leave her also hanging on her cross, suffering, and there would be no escape from it. This view of life felt very disturbing, she said. It shattered the reverie of a happier, idyllic world created by a positive God who protected people from suffering if they lived according to her

God's moral law. This was the world into which she escaped to avoid the anxiety that might arise in her at the hands of her father with his threatening dark moods and explosive anger as well as her mother's passive-aggressive jealousy.

The dreamer talked at some length about her childhood and what she now acknowledged to be her defenses against the anxiety always lurking in the background of her daily life. "But," she said, "last night I had a strangely enjoyable and comforting dream." This was her dream:

> *I am enjoying a wonderful conversation with an*
> *elderly man who says his name is Gita.*

She remembered nothing else except that the conversation was so meaningful that, when she woke up, she tried to go back to sleep and reconnect with the dream.

I asked, "Who is Gita? What do you associate to him?"

Her answer surprised me: "The *Bhagavad Gita*"! My surprise was because the dreamer had never indicated any interest in other religions or world cultures. Fascinated with her response, I asked her how she knew about the *Bhagavad Gita*, one of the holiest books in Hinduism.

To my continued surprise, she told me the following story. As a child, she lived in the county, growing up outside her relatively small rural town. But when she entered high school, each day at the end of classes she would walk to the county library a few blocks away and read until 5:00 p.m., when her mother would conclude her secretarial work and drive by the library to take the two of them home. She read many interesting books in the adult section, she told me, and one of her more interesting discoveries was the *Bhagavad Gita*.

Her understanding of the Hindu holy book was quite superficial, as might be expected from a 15-year-old, which was her age when she read the book more than 40 years ago. It had to do, she said, with religion, yoga, and life.

"What about Krishna?" I asked.

Out popped another surprise with that question. "Oh, yes, I just remembered. When I finished college, moved into my first apartment, and got a cat, I named him Krishna!"

But she did not know who Krishna was, nor Arjuna (a main character), nor the basic plot of the *Bhagavad Gita*. However, she was interested in learning about the book: how it means "The Song of God" and that it deals with the meaning of human existence and the responsibility of facing the suffering of one's duty in life. It explains how the brave warrior Arjuna felt he could not face the epic battle about to take place among his kinsmen even though he was a strong warrior and the fact that Krishna was an incarnation of the Supreme God of the universe in Hindu religion. Krishna urged Arjuna to suffer his responsibilities with the assurance that Krishna would be with him in life and in death.

As in my dreamer's conversation with Gita in her dream, she seemed to be enthralled with the themes of the

Bhagavad Gita, especially the idea of facing suffering but not being overwhelmed by it. "Several things are going on in my mind," she said.

I will summarize her thoughts as she reported them: First, she found some kind of comfort that the act of suffering was dealt with in such a profound, universal way within a culture and religion of another place and time. Second, she was astonished that a dream could come to her at a time of her deep need with an offering of insight that would bring comfort. Third, she stood in awe witnessing the working of her psyche. It could hold in memory a reference to an obscure book she read more than 45 years earlier, when she was a naïve teenager, and now manifest that memory as a dream image in the form of a wisdom figure such as Gita. "This," she said, "is awesome."

Finally, I had the sense that this encounter with the God-image of another culture—although in a dream—helped her to deepen her own Christian understanding of God. It opened the door to her instinctual life (represented in her reported first dream's two snakes). Although she was standing at the threshold of integrating her instinctual and spiritual life, the naïveté of her Sunday School theology yielded to a more mature realization of the deeper Mystery within which we live, move, and have our being.

But it is also that within which, and of which, each of us dreams.

WHEN YOU COME TO THE FORK IN THE ROAD

Yogi Berra seems not to have had a problem with the fork in the road. He said simply, "When you come to the fork in the road, take it."

Were it so simple! But it's not. We come to the proverbial "fork in the road" many times in our lives and cannot simply "take it" because we—unlike Yogi—face a choice.

We face a choice, either "this" way or "that" way, and each one seems to be equally appealing, or on the other hand, equally unappealing. And sometimes the seeming consequences of our decision paralyze us. We may feel overwhelmed at the thought of what we may lose if we make the wrong decision. Or perhaps even more disturbing is that situation we face when we know that any decision we make will result in having to give up something too important to lose. Here we face stalemate: We cannot decide.

So here it is, the "either-or" of life, the fork in the road that brings us to the moment of truth in our existence when we face a difficult choice. Do you remember that horrifying scene in the movie *Sophie's Choice* (1982), in which a sadistic Nazi officer forces a Polish immigrant mother, sent to the Auschwitz concentration camp of World War II, to face the unbearable decision of choosing which of her two children will live? It is a searing scene that exposes us to the hellish evil that human beings can impose on others.

And I am happy to realize with you that the great majority of us will likely never have to face such a choice as Sophie's. However, as I was saying earlier, the choices we do have to face may feel tinged with the chilling hint of a foreboding dilemma forced upon us that we will do all within our power to avoid. We postpone the decision, we try not to think about it, or we attempt to distract ourselves in unhealthy ways of acting out so that we can cover up the approaching decision with some fleeting feel-good experience.

Think about it. Consider how we like to think that the good times of the present will last forever. And then we go around the curve of life's path and discover an approaching fork in the road: a new job, a transfer, a relocation, a tantalizing relationship, a medical decision, a change in our life situation brought on by aging, an accident, or a fluctuation in the Dow Jones. Sometimes even the positive developments in our lives bring on an unanticipated fork in the road. We inherit a lot of money, graduate with a prestigious degree after years of hard work when it seemed impossible, fall in love with a partner we feared did not exist, or perhaps have a child who succeeds in some facet of life and fills us with joy but requires a change in our priorities of spending and following other dreams.

So it goes. These developments fall within the areas I have called the five fundamental questions of life:

(1) Who am I? (2) Where do I belong? (3) Where am I to go? (4) What shall I do? (5) Why?

You will notice that they all have to do with choices.

1. WHO AM I?

This is the question of identity. Here is the problem. My identity changes daily even as I remain the same person! How can it be otherwise? I age and circumstances change all around me in my circle of family, friends, acquaintances, and world dynamics. I make mistakes, learn, and, hopefully, grow, and as I do so, I change. My appearance changes. If you have forgotten or not accepted how much you have changed, just go back to your high school's 50th reunion! That's right, those "old people" you see sitting in the hotel's banquet hall? Those are your old classmates who are not alone in their changes in appearance! But it's not just appearance. When you listen to their stories, you hear most fascinating things and occasionally a story that truly astounds. Someone you knew to be the most-likely-to-succeed has not been successful at all, and the one you thought to be a ne'er-do-well has accomplished more than you ever have or will! Go figure. Yes, our identities change, more than we may realize, and then we look in the mirror and ask: Who am I?

2. WHERE DO I BELONG?

This is the question of community. I am talking here about all those groups in which we enclose ourselves: family, religious affiliations, clubs, social groups, political parties, geographical regions, or nationalities, for example. It is a part of our nature to belong to social structures. It is also the nature of some groups, organizations, or families to demand and expect uncompromising loyalty. In fact, our identities are closely tied to these groups. We identify with specific social structures until we do not, and then the problem occurs. I change, circumstances change, and then I sense a shift in the groups to which I want to belong. Even family loyalties evolve in unexpected directions for some of us. We sense we no longer fit in as we once did, and the fork in the road appears: Where do I belong?

3. WHERE AM I TO GO?

This is the question of life's direction, or vocation. Once again, you will see the connection between the first two questions and this third one. You begin to see here the inter-penetrating nature of these questions. One influences all, and they all influence each single one, because my vocation will be strongly influenced by my background and participation in family life and the various social groups to which I have belonged. But it is also true that we as individuals strike out on our own, so to speak. We hear an inner voice or encounter some person, event, or place that speaks to us, and we know: "This is my calling. This is the direction in which I must head." But it may seem to be too risky, too challenging, or too unacceptable to people whose opinions I value, or the "call" may come at an inconvenient time in my life. I face a choice: Where am I to go?

4. WHAT SHOULD I DO?

Here we come to the question of our morality. I am looking here at something deeper than an organization's code of ethics, as important as that may be, or the family of origin's way of behaving, as positive as it might possibly be. In other words, it becomes an easy matter to follow the "playbook" of our family or social group or workplace, and to do so without ever coming to grasps with my own moral code. The way I think, speak, act, and work may be very disconnected as far as my morality is concerned. I may act one way at home and another way at work. To return to the movie *Sophie's Choice* and the behavior of the Nazi officer who acted so cruelly toward Sophie and her children, it reminds us of stories of Nazi officials who did the most despicable things in their work but who then returned home as loving, sensitive, compassionate fathers and husbands. Such a life is compartmentalized. This is easy for us to do in our world today where the bottom line of making money for a corporation may lead us to adopt a "leadership" style praised in the workplace but completely contrary to one's private and personal beliefs and values. However, something may happen, something crosses our path, and we get a notion of discontent in which we see the incompatibility of our lifestyle with who we want to be on the inside. We then face a choice: What should I do?

5. WHY?

I have formulated this question in the simplest way I know to express what I believe to be a matter of deep spirituality. This question arises from the human spirit that longs to look underneath the other questions. In other words, our identities, communities, vocations, and moral patterns become rigid; they no longer serve life and our potential to realize the truth of our being. Life does not stand still. Bidden or not bidden, recognized or not, choices arrive at our door each day calling for decisions that may not come easily or lightly. That is the problem. As Yogi Berra's simplistic approach suggests, when we come to the fork in the road, we may indeed take it with no thought at all, or we may not even recognize it as a fork! We simply "keep on keeping on" even though life may be calling for us to make some significant change or to recommit to what we are doing, but in a more conscious way.

This is the deep longing of the human spirit, to become conscious. And it is the "fork in the road" that is placed there to awaken us from our slumber, our way of driving on "automatic pilot." It is the fork in the road that leads us to pause and take stock. Who are we? Where do we belong? What direction should we take? What should we do? Why?

And then a dream appears.

CHAPTER
TWO

SYMBOLS

*Symbols are images or objects that represent something
whose meaning and significance cannot be fully
communicated, in contrast to a sign whose meaning
is clearly understood. A country's flag is a symbol,
and a traffic directional signal is a sign.*
—*R. Mishoe*

THE ULTIMATE QUESTION

My friend described in his email a "big" issue he was pondering having to do with our expanding population and dwindling resources. He raised questions he found to be important and invited me to ponder with him what he referred to as the "big" issues of our day.

This friend—a community psychologist and anthropologist, retired and living abroad where he last taught in a university—now enjoys the leisure of prodding me and others with information he digs out of his regular scans of the World Wide Web. He is a delight to be with, stimulating, funny, insightful, and always a provocateur who nudges people toward thinking outside their comfort zones.

But his email came at a time I was pondering other matters. For instance, it has come to me that the "big" issues and questions are not the same as the "ultimate" issues and questions; nor, for that matter, are they the same as another group I would call "immediate" issues and questions.

The issues in the "immediate" category have to do with the daily and regular concerns of home, relationships, work, and finances—all important enough that they may feel "big" in the anxiety they can stir. Likewise, the "big" issues and questions can (and should) concern us to the point where we become informed citizens of the world, engaging the perplexing challenges facing our planet in matters of environment, religious extremism, economic collapse, population growth, the widening gulf between rich and poor, and so much more. We will not sit idly by while these catastrophic scenarios perform their dance of death boldly before us.

But these are not the ultimate issues, are they? And, in fact, if we cannot or will not ask these ultimate questions, we will very likely fail in asking the big and immediate ones.

So, what are these ultimate questions? I have no doubt you can supply your own list if you pause for just a moment to think about them—as I had been prompted to do when my friend sent his email.

What prompted, my thinking about the nature of the ultimate question was a date that popped up on my calendar: June 26, the birthday of Carl Jung. For some reason, I came to think about his visit to the Athi Plains of Nairobi, Africa, in the autumn of 1925. There, in a broad savanna, with no sight or sound of another human being, walking a little distance by himself from his camp, he experienced what he called "the stillness of the eternal beginning, the world as it had always been … ." There, in that eternal silence, he could hear the question within himself: What is our [humanity's] myth? In other words, he was asking what it is that human beings bring to this world. Why are we here?

As so often may happen, I found myself asking another question, one that I first encountered in the writings of Paul Tillich, a major theologian of the 20th century. That question—"Why is there something and not nothing?"—probably originated with the Greek philosopher Parmenides in the 5th century B.C.E.

I realize that the question may sound to our ears as contrived or speculatively wasteful of our time because any answer will likely satisfy only the person who attempts an answer. But, as with most ultimate questions, its significance lies in the asking and not the answering. When we remember where Tillich was when he asked that question in desperation, we may then pause to ask it for ourselves.

Tillich was a philosopher/theologian with a keen intellect as well as a formal and informal education that served his mind very well. Born in 1880 in Starzeddel, a village near Berlin, Germany, Tillich was ordained as a Lutheran minister but planned to become a professor. He volunteered to serve as a chaplain in the German army in World War I, believing in "a nice God who would make everything turn out for the best," only to find himself breaking down after prolonged service under deadly enemy fire. From the hospital where he recuperated before returning to the front lines, he wrote his family of the terrible catastrophe and "the end of the world order," as he faced almost certain death in the trenches. "Why is there something and not nothing?" Tillich found at that time he had no answer but a koan-like question.

But is it not the case with all ultimate questions that they redirect our thinking? Jesus of Nazareth asks, "So what does it profit anyone to gain the whole world and lose their soul?" Or as the Buddha simply put it, "What is suffering?" Jesus responds to his question by pointing toward another realm of reality, the Kingdom of Heaven, which intersects this worldly order. This may not satisfy you, nor may the Buddha's preaching of the Four Noble Truths and the Noble Eightfold Path. Still, their questions remain, and they may bring us into the creative sphere of a meditative silence, if heard through the clatter of the cacophony playing in our minds.

However, at times the ultimate question intersects the big and immediate ones, such as when I arrive home and my wife greets me, after she's had a particularly grueling day at work, with this question: "What do you think about Chinese takeout tonight?" That is immediate, it's really big, and I can see in her eyes it's ultimately important I answer this one right!

WHAT IS "IT?"

I magine this. It is late at night, and a baby lying in her nursery room begins to cry. Hearing her baby cry, the mother wakes up and rushes to the crib. She picks up the baby, holds the child close to her breast, rocks gently while rubbing the infant's back, and softly assures the baby with these words: "It's alright; it's alright."

You know this experience I am describing quite well. You yourself have been there, either to repeat the very same ritual, or you know about it. You understand "It" and empathize with "It." You know that "It" is an act repeated around the world many times each night in the households of all peoples, all countries, all ethnic groups, and all religions.

But step back from this experience just a moment and think with me. Just what does the mother or father mean when she/he picks up the frightened child and says, "It's alright." What is "It?" Is "It" a supposed object of fear or pain? Is "It" a reference to something specific that the parent knows might frighten or disturb the child?

37

In some instances, this may be the case, but probably not in most. No, I think the statement, "It's alright," points to something much deeper. I think this is one of the most fundamental, universal statements of faith. I believe the parent's assurance precedes any doctrinaire creed, any formulation of orthodoxy, any "reasoned" response to life's questions of existence. The quiet utterance of comfort to the anxious child leads back to the early dawn of human life and points over the horizon of our future toward whatever may be the most humane of responses that we will ever offer our children in distress.

To say "It's alright" is a statement of faith that indirectly assures the child with the following affirmations:

~ Yes, the universe is basically a purposive home in which we are welcome to belong and live our lives;

~ Yes, we can trust life as a wonderful experience that will offer us an abundance of joy, fulfillment, and meaning—even with all the suffering we experience;

~ Yes, this darkness will pass and tomorrow we may enjoy the sunlight of another day;

~ Yes, there are wonderful people who will love you, care for you, and hold your hand as long as you live;

~ Yes, there will be serendipitous surprises to greet you each day and fill your lifetime with

worthwhile challenges and opportunities to join
in creating an even more marvelous planet on
which to live;

~ Yes, you will grow old and know pain and die,
but you will also know the greatest joy of saying
at the end that you would not have had it any
other way;

~ Yes, I am here with you, for you, and you
will never know a day that you do not feel my
presence and rest assured of my belief in you.

Is that not "It?" Is that not what the mother most deeply
is offering her child, most steadfastly believing at that anxious
moment of offering comfort, most courageously striving to
see that such a world will be made possible for her child?
Of course, it is. But, yes, of course, we lose our way. The
baby grows up, becomes a teenager. Stuff happens to us. We
become distant, maybe, if indeed not callous, cold, bitter,
beaten-down.

But in the deeper recesses of our mind, "It" remains.
"It" will never be completely erased because "It" is the true
heritage of our existence on this planet. The great religions
remind us of "It." The philosophers help us to find words to
describe "It." The highest courts of civil society protect the
rights of all people to seek "It." And deep within our souls
we believe "It" is essentially what we want for all people. If
you do not believe "It," just observe any grandparent who

unabashedly points to their grandchild as proof of life's evolution toward "greatness" and proof that "It" is true and worth any effort!

Still, you may be thinking, there is the shadow side of "It." There is suffering; there are unspeakable things that also move in the darkness of human existence. We have seen many lives wasted. Many people who once were held by their mothers and assured "It's alright" have not found that assurance to be their birthright, or at least they were never able to claim "It."

This is indeed the case. Within the mysterious shadows of our existence, suffering has a way of exposing us to the four-fold experiences of disease, old age, death, and meaninglessness. Those are the big four. They are awesome, and they are the sub-themes of my musings.

TRACKING YOUR PERSONAL MYTH

I t is interesting that one of the first questions coming to mind when we meet a stranger is, "What do you do?" True, quite often the job one does tells a lot about the person—but not all. And, certainly, one's work does not say much about the depth of character of that individual.

Of course, "not-knowing" works very well in a populated, busy world such as ours. We do not have the time—or interest—to go deep in our conversations with people. The anecdote is told about the prominent theologian Paul Tillich, who was rescued from Nazi Germany through the strong efforts of Reinhold Niebuhr and others. They made possible a professorship for Tillich in Manhattan at Union Theological Seminary, which in turn also made available a faculty apartment for Tillich and his wife. However, not always understanding the nuances of his new language, Tillich occasionally would not catch the real meaning of a very commonplace English expression, such as the greeting, "How are you?" It is said that as he left his apartment in the early morning on his way to his office, other faculty members soon learned not to ask him, "How are you?" When asked, Tillich would proceed to tell them in great detail how he felt, how he slept, any pains he might be experiencing in his body, and so forth.

So, yes, we can sometimes know more than we want or need to know about another person's life. We do not necessarily need to know the other person's personal myth, but I am suggesting that it is valuable to know our own for the following reasons.

First, I am aware that even the word *myth* is a problem for many people. As it is used in our everyday language, most often it connotes something not true, a fiction, an ancient story to describe the exploits of gods and goddesses of prehistoric people and places. However, *myth* may be used today in reference to a "symbolical story" (*Oxford Dictionary*). As such, myth does something nothing else does. As a symbolical story, myth provides a meaningful narrative that helps to "make sense" of a people, a geographical locale, a country, a group of people, or an individual. A myth may have a collective meaning or a very personal one; sometimes it seems that the two may be entwined.

And, as you might expect, I am drawing significantly on the life and work of Carl Jung to throw light on our process of tracking our personal myths. For it is indeed a very psychological experience. As Jung puts it:

> *... the right way to wholeness is made up, unfort-*
> *nately, of fateful detours and wrong turnings. It*
> *is a longissima via, not straight but snakelike, a*
> *path that unites the opposites in the manner of the*
> *guiding caduceus, a path whose labyrinthine twists*
> *and turns are not lacking terrors. (CW 12, para. 6)*

One might say that the "path to wholeness" is the "track" to one's personal myth. In other words, it is the journey, not the destination, that matters. And the track will probably lead through the narrow pass where the "opposites" threaten to collide, across the dark ocean of anxiety where we hear strange voices in the depths, and into the lonely desert where there are no road signs. In fact, if our journey does not have something of those features, then it probably is not the track to our personal myth. More than likely, it is the well-worn collective interstate that leads to Anytown, USA (substitute your country), and a "life of more of the same." As Robert Frost said in "The Road Not Taken":

> *Two roads diverged in a wood, and I—*
> *I took the one less traveled by,*
> *And that has made all the difference.*

Granted, Frost's poem has been analyzed and debated for decades, and even Frost himself reflected a strange ambiguity regarding its meaning. But that is more to my point: There is a traveling, a journeying, a tracking, or—if you will—a seeking to discern our true star that is experienced by most human beings, provided we have not been so wounded by trauma, poverty, illiteracy, and cynicism that we have lost the very human yearning for a meaning that fulfills and completes our unique life.

I say "unique" life because there is no other life like yours. It is true that there are archetypal patterns of experience that are universal. We recognize something of our path in the lives of other people, living or dead. But, like our unique fingerprints, like the unique snowflake, there is no one else identical to you. And that is why it is your personal myth, your seeking for wholeness in the complex make-up of your personality, and your search for meaning that can only be stated through a symbolical story woven from dreams, fantasies, defeats, victories, struggles, encounters, and an opportunity to "connect the dots."

In his autobiography, *Memories, Dreams, Reflections*, Jung opens his Prologue like this:

> *My life is a story of the self-realization of the uncon-*
> *scious. Everything in the unconscious seeks outward*
> *manifestation, and the personality too desires to*
> *evolve out of its unconscious conditions and to*
> *experience itself as a whole. …*
> *What we are to our inward vision, and what man*

appears to be sub specie aeternitatis, can only be
expressed by way of myth. Myth is more individual
and expresses life more precisely than does science.
… Thus it is that I have now undertaken, in my
eighty-third year, to tell my personal myth. I can
only make direct statements, only "tell stories."
Whether or not the stories are "true" is not the
problem. The only question is whether what I tell
is my fable, my truth. (MDR, p. 3)

Unlike many of us, Carl Jung seemed to have begun tracking his personal myth quite young. At least, he traces his first dream back to age 3 and goes from there. Even so, it was not until after many dreams, many adventures, travels, highs and lows, successes and failures that he could say with certainty in 1927, at age 52, that he recognized his own journeying toward his personal myth, climaxing with the dream of a magnolia tree with reddish blossoms in the middle of an island, situated within a city square in Liverpool.

We also have dreams. And on some level, even if it is unconscious, we are tracking our personal myths. Some part of us is trying to make sense of our meanderings, to find meaning in the dreams and experiences of waking life with all their fateful encounters and symbolic narratives. Meanwhile, we excuse ourselves with lesser stories that we are too busy, too tired, too distracted, too old, too young, or too sick. Or we may indeed be caught under the compelling power of outer myths that urge us to make money, enlist in the army of doing-good, seek refuge in the ten-thousand diversions that promise to entertain us, make us look better, bring us happiness, or hold the key to the secret of life.

These too may become our personal myths, and maybe they serve us well. But we must ask: Is the story of this myth complete? Does the myth hold you within the tension of your fragmented parts in the service of becoming whole? Does the myth carry you so that the movement of your life outside and inside leads to experiences of meaning, wisdom, reverence, and gratitude, enabling you to face death knowing you have lived *your* life and not that of someone else?

If not, you probably have fallen into a dysfunctional myth. Think about the biker whose tattoo proclaims, "Born to Lose." That may be his/her personal myth, but it is a dysfunctional one. The example, of course, is extreme, but you get the point. Just because you know the plot very well and have memorized your lines does not mean the story is personally yours. Maybe it happened to be the only one you thought available, but no longer is this so.

In other words, the darkness around us is deep, the ways are many, and the shrill voices call us from every corner. But take heart: Our dreams do not lie, and the markers for our track are those symbols that will make us whole. When all else has finished and nothing else remains, what you will treasure most is your Story and those symbols that brought light to the darkness of your great uncertainties.

EVIL: THOUGHTS FOLLOWING THE CRASH OF THE JETLINER

The crash of the Germanwings Airbus A320 in the French Alps on March 24, 2015, held the world in horrified suspense and then shock upon learning details about the last eight minutes of the plane's flight. In several subdued conversations with people following the plane's crash, along with news reports that it was very likely a mass murder-suicide at the hands of the copilot, I kept hearing questions about mental illness and the nature of evil as people tried to understand the terrifying and senseless tragedy. What follows are some of my thoughts at this moment when I also am caught in the collective experience of shock, grief, anger, disbelief, and puzzlement.

I seem to need to revisit the subject of evil. Perhaps it will be helpful to hold up alongside the Germanwings' plane crash other tragedies that prompt associations with evil. These accounts of human suffering fall into the following categories: natural evil, systemic evil, moral evil, and the archetype of evil.

But before I begin that grouping, I will offer a working definition of evil. From the *New Oxford American Dictionary* comes this definition:

- "profoundly immoral and malevolent;"
- "(of a force or spirit) embodying or associated with the forces of the devil;"
- "harmful or intending to harm;"
- "(of something seen or smelled) extremely unpleasant."

All of these are adjectives. Nouns include the following:

- "profound immorality, wickedness, and depravity, esp. when regarded as a supernatural force;"
- "a manifestation of this, esp. in people's actions;"
- "something that is harmful or undesirable."

With those working definitions, I begin my groupings.

NATURAL EVIL

With earthquakes, tsunamis, floods, volcanoes, fires, tornadoes, hurricanes, etc., entire villages may be destroyed, natural habitats ruined, properties lost, even geographical boundaries changed forever, and thousands of human and animal lives lost. The suffering in those situations is without measure. The same holds true for disease, genetic malformations, and catastrophic illness. Lives are wasted, families are overwhelmed, and life's savings are erased.

We cannot escape the calamitous consequences of these events. Nor are they in any way respective of race, religion, economic status, or locality. We live in a world of unpredictable natural disasters and experience them directly ourselves, in the lives of people we know, or among those we see on our TV screens.

There was a time when the monotheistic faiths may have attributed these natural disasters either to willful acts of God as punishment of some sort; or, secondly, the events might have been attributed to the work of the devil, Satan, or demons acting on behalf of those fiendish powers. Gradually, however, we are coming to understand that in a universe of freedom, bad things do happen to good people, and we do not resort to labeling our catastrophes as acts of God. We are free from that—but not quite. For example, even our legal, financial, and insurance systems may still refer to natural catastrophes as "acts of God" (and this promulgates the idea of evil as having come from the hands of an idiosyncratic deity!). Some individuals know better and yet still fall into the old trap of viewing God as the cause of all natural suffering. Hardly a month goes by that someone in my consulting room does not ask, in regard to some experience of suffering, "Why is God doing this to me?" The old view of a tyrannical deity whose main function is to reward and punish people—those views are anchored deeply in the subterranean recesses of our deep psyches.

SYSTEMIC EVIL

This is the face of evil that Hannah Arendt may have called banal. In her 1963 book, *Eichmann in Jerusalem*, Arendt described the role of Adolf Eichmann in following Hitler's order to eliminate the Jews of Europe. She focused on what she perceived to be Eichmann's bureaucratic mentality as the banality of evil by which monstrous actions followed the countless details of institutional decisions that ultimately led to the death camps where five million to six million Jews died in the Holocaust, labeled simply as the "Final Solution."

Nothing I say will match the barbaric slaughter of the Holocaust, and I mean to do no disservice to that event by listing other examples of human suffering in the same category. They may be of lesser importance in the minds of some, but who can say? Such so-called banality of evil can live among us and might come to our full attention only later.

Think, for example, of the slave ships that brought people of African descent to our shores where they existed in a servitude that resembled a living death, the aftereffects of which still haunt us today and tear apart our people. This is the way of all "isms": racism, sexism, ageism. It is the way also of so much collective and corporate life in which persons are treated like chattel, objects to be used, abused, moved around, and discarded as impersonal means toward profitable ends. Consider how in the Great Recession of 2008, the big institutions of money and power caught up individuals and smaller groups in a bureaucratic game of high-stakes monopoly. Everyone sought to become rich with little thought to the excesses that crashed on top of the paper empire, driving people's personal properties under water and losing the small life savings of others.

I am reminded of a theme in John Steinbeck's *The Grapes of Wrath* (1939). The farmer is desperate for a loan to keep his farm and looks to the bank that professes it would like to accommodate the request personally, but the bank's policy will not allow such a loan as it must answer to others who control it "back East." To this, Steinbeck writes in chapter five:

> *The bank is something else than men. It happens*
> *that every man in a bank hates what the bank does,*
> *and yet the bank does it.*
> *The bank is something more than men, I tell you.*
> *It's the monster.*
> *Men made it, but they can't control it.*

This is the innocuous but destructive banality of evil in which people become trapped systemically to commit acts they want to believe are not of their own doing. All acts of systemic evil begin in the safe fortress of our extremist views, whether they be patriotism, religious fundamentalism, an unregulated capitalism, or an over-regulated socialism.

MORAL EVIL

But here we come to that dimension of evil in which we see our own hand most clearly. In a much-studied experiment by the Yale University psychologist Stanley Milgram, reported in his 1974 book, *Obedience to Authority*, Milgram reports on an experiment described briefly as follows. Individuals participated in administering what they thought to be electrical shocks to another participant in the experiment who was actually an actor pretending to be experiencing the pain of increasing levels of voltage.

What Milgram reported in his study, and this has been duplicated in several subsequent experiments, was that a great majority of individuals, when instructed by the "authority" conducting the process to administer the painful levels of voltage, complied with the instructions even though they believed they were inflicting great pain on another person and, as Milgram states in his book, had no hostility toward the other individual.

The findings of this study supposedly reveal how susceptible persons are to committing destructive acts under the conditions of being instructed to do so by "authorities." The focus here seemed to concentrate on the role of the authorities in leading persons to harm others. But that shadow side of human personality has an even greater window for violent acts to emerge. Think of what individuals can do when they fear for their survival, when they dislike other persons and feel threatened by them, when they are jealous, when they think that for whatever reason they deserve or are entitled to cut corners and get what they want. Psychoanalysis has helped reveal to us how vulnerable we are to the unconscious dynamics of projection of evil upon others, of compartmentalizing our lives and rationalizing, and demonizing others. Each of us is capable of these patterns by which the little betrayals become great acts of evil. "Oh what tangled webs we weave when first we practice to deceive," says Walter Scott in *Marmion*. Under the most convoluted cloud of self-deception, believing ourselves to be protectors of virtue, we let slip the shadow life of our worst selves.

THE ARCHETYPE OF EVIL

And the prince of darkness, the archetype of evil, is the devil that dwells within our deep psyche, or the collective unconscious, as Jung named it. It is this prince of darkness who commands our worst selves and who sets loose the fires of destruction that erupt into wars, famine, pestilence, and death. It is this force, the archetype of evil, that functions in our personalities and erupts in our external world as the autonomous spirit of evil that may inhabit persons and groups and nations.

I am well aware that this language may be offensive to some and embraced by others, but in any case, the language is not foreign to us. Either as religious reality, hypostasis, or metaphor, the idea of the "devil" holds a place in our language, literature, and imagination. Look again at the definition given by the *Oxford American Dictionary* with which I began.

What do I make of it? As a nontheist, I certainly do not regard the "devil" as a being that haunts our world and delivers us to the hell of everlasting fire and damnation. So I turn to the two sources that have informed me most regarding human nature and the nature of evil.

The first source is that of the New Testament world shaped by Greek thought and synthesized in the Judeo-Christian heritage that has given us those scriptures. In those texts, there are several words used to describe evil as something bad, but only one word describing evil as an active, autonomous agency or principle (see John Sanford's *Mystical Christianity*, 1997). That word is *poneros*, used to refer either to the "Evil One" or to evil as a force in itself.

We must be careful here, because again, this does not refer to a being rambling about in the world. This is a description of a psychic dynamic. It is what Jung called an archetype. You could call it the archetype of the devil, or the evil one, or the shadow, or the adversary, or the power of non-being. Remember, an archetype is an "innate neuropsychic center possessing the capacity to initiate, control and mediate the common behavioral characteristics and typical characteristics of all human beings irrespective of race, culture or creed" (Stevens, 2003, p. 352). In other words, and in everyday language, the "archetype of evil" is nothing less or more than what people have meant when they said—in humor or in sincerity—"the devil made me do it." That is to say, in our common wisdom, we know indeed that there are occasions when "something comes over us" or "something gets into us," and in those experiences it is as if we are taken over by a foreign power in the service of destruction.

This is our psychological legacy. It informs our notions of evil and makes more understandable our experiences of natural, systemic, and moral evil. Such an understanding of evil brings us to a gravitas in which we regard our encounters with evil as nothing less than an assault against the principle of life, the encounter of Being with the dark force of Non-Being, in which all possibilities for happiness, hope, reverence, and ecstasy hang suspended, awaiting the outcome.

THE MYSTERIOUS UNIVERSE:
DARK HOLES, GOD, AND THE
TAO OF SYNCHRONICITY

D id you hear the chirping sound that was 1.2 billion years old? I am aware you expect a joke to follow unless you read the subsequent news about the sound made when two black holes (dying stars) collapsed into each other and formed the mega-black hole which, had the light been visible, would be equal to the brightness of a billion trillion suns! Even before their dance of approaching death, one of the black holes was 39 times the size of our sun, and the other dying star was 29 times the size of our sun. (For this and other information, see Dennis Overbye's article, "Gravitational Waves Detected, Confirming Einstein's Theory," in *The New York Times,* February 11, 2016.)

The sound to which I referred above was detected by the mammoth listening device called a "Laser Interferometer Gravitational Wave" antenna, designed to pick up the sounds

of so-called "ripples of space-time," another name for gravitational waves. These "ripples" of space-time had been hypoth-
esized by Albert Einstein 100 years earlier as the "body" of
our universe. This body, he thought, could be shaped and
contorted much like a bed's mattress would be if you threw
a rock in the mattress, only in this instance the contortion
of the gravitational waves, or "ripples," was caused by a kind
of apocalyptic collapse of two dying stars caught within the
gravitational pull of the bodies, each circling the other.

That is my layman's description of the cosmic event that
caught the attention of scientists around the world, as well as
many of us who continue to try to understand astral physics,
quantum and gravitational fields, and Einstein's theory of
relativity. What is immediately significant about this and of
value to you and me in our everyday life?

Let me give you an example. While I pondered the news
of those black holes colliding into each other, rippling the
gravitational waves of the universe and uttering a sound we
heard 1.2 billion light years later, a sound registered as middle
C in our music scale—while I thought about the utter awe-
someness of the event and the equally awesome fact that we
could pick up that sound, an interesting thing happened
to me. I had just picked up my pen to write this blog. At
that moment, I knew only that the black-hole event seemed
important to me in some way that had not become clear.

Then, just as I had written the title of the blog and the
first paragraph, I received an email. All the way over on the

other side of the globe, in Australia, my friend sent me a message with the subject line: "A wow experience—stunning time lapse will make you see the heavens in a whole new light."

"See the heavens in a whole new light" ... that was exactly my experience of the two black holes colliding, emitting a sound we could hear 1.2 billion years later. It confirmed Einstein's theory regarding the shape of the universe as it might shift its form in response to the pattern of gravitational waves and thereby change space and time as well. Just the idea itself that space and time are conditioned by the changing patterns of gravitational waves strains my understanding. In addition, to receive a message from a friend on the other side of the planet, a message having to do with the ways we see and experience the universe, that also strains my understanding. My friend and I had not been messaging each other about the universe and its mysteries. Also, his message was not at all about the black holes but about the way we see and experience the universe.

This so-called "coincidence" of events is in itself a mystery. And it happens more frequently than we think. For example, I wake up thinking about an old friend I have not talked with in more than five years, and then the phone rings. It is my friend who happened to be thinking of me. This experience of so-called coincidences is what Jung named "synchronicity."

By synchronicity, Jung meant the meaningful experience of events that coincide in space and time for which there is no explanation of cause and effect. This is not telepathic communication between persons because there can be synchronistic events that do not occur between two or more persons, but also between persons and other objects. One example frequently cited is the "Pauli Effect." This refers to the reported tendency of laboratory experimental equipment to break regularly when the theoretical physicist Wolfgang Pauli came into close proximity with such equipment. (See George Gamow's account of this in his book, *Thirty Years That Shook Physics: The Story of Quantum Theory,* p. 64.)

Jung's understanding of synchronicity is that there is a connection in the universe between all things. In his essay *Synchronicity: An Acausal Connecting Principle (CW 8),* Jung attempts to link the academic islands of psychology, philosophy, religion, and science by sketching the parameters of synchronicity as a "field" of meaningful connectivity that operates within the universe in addition to the quantum field, the magnetic-gravitational field, and the field of gravity.

My "take-away" from all this might be summarized with the following statements:

1. You and I are connected in ways we do not comprehend.

2. Occasions pop up in our lives when we may become aware of our connection in a meaningful way, a "synchronicity."

3. So it is throughout the universe that there exists a web of connectivity that cannot fully be explained by our present scientific paradigms.

4. This underlying process of connectedness seems to be what the Chinese philosophers call the *TAO*, defined by the *American Heritage Dictionary* as "… the basic, eternal principle of the universe that transcends reality, and is the source of being, non-being, and change." It may also be called the "Ground of Being," a term given us by the theologian/philosopher Paul Tillich to refer to "God," the ultimate source of all.

These are my statements. I offer them as someone who ponders the mystery of the universe with increasing marvel at the meaningful connections. At the same time, I am very aware of the danger of apophenia, the tendency to see meaningful connections or patterns where there are none because of the need to see those patterns. This brings its own danger, however, and that is the tendency to see a pattern of no connections because we believe there could be none. This would perhaps be most tragic of all. How sad to be fully alive with another and not to realize the connection.

PLAYING GOD IN THE TECHNOCOMPLEX:
WHEN OUR OBSESSION WITH TECHNOLOGY BECOMES AN ALLIANCE WITH THE DEVIL

HOMO SAPIEN: The species of bipedal primates to which modern humans belong, characterized by a brain capacity averaging 1400 cc (85 cu in.) and by dependence upon language and the creation and utilization of complex tools.
(Random House Kernerman Webster's College Dictionary)

TECHNOCOMPLEX: A state of mind characterized by a fascination with the potential, mystery, and power of technological creations, especially of high-technology, leading to a condition of obsession, preoccupation, and/or dependency upon these tools to the neglect of other human values.
(R. Mishoe, 2016)

I begin this blog with the definitions in order to underline the point I am making concerning humanity's relation to the tools we have created. Going back to the first definition of *Homo sapien,* what stands out is the third of our distinguishing characteristics. The first is our brain size, the second is our use of and dependency upon language, but the third characteristic is one we do not often think about: "the creation and utilization of complex tools."

One such tool is the smartphone. We cannot put the thing down. We take it everywhere, pull it out the first moment we have free, interrupt our conversations with friends and business associates to answer a call or to make one, and now use it for everything—directions, music, information about complex matters, photography, etc., etc.

It is not that we have phones but that they have us. We approach panic when we think we may have lost our phone, and we eagerly wait for the new revised phone that will make our present one obsolete. Our dependency upon this device grows daily.

That's just the phone. Now look around at all the other gadgets that help us do our work, entertain us, provide medical services, and—oh, yes—take us places! Our automobiles are becoming smarter with each year, and already they have more computers than our astronauts had to go to the moon, and we may only be going grocery shopping.

But you know all this. It has become commonplace to go on and on with others about our dependency upon our gadgets. However, lurking in the background of our conversation is a growing awareness or even apprehension about the speed with which these high-tech gadgets are becoming smarter than we are. It is as if we have created something that is now re-making the world in which we live, toward what end we do not know.

Whether it is a blessing or a curse may depend. Whether or not we are co-creating a world in which the treasures of our humanity are left behind, on behalf of a conjured power that will possess us, may depend upon how conscious we are about our fascination with this newly found power, a malicious power emerging from our unconscious alliance with a soul-less technology that tempts us with god-like attributes of omnipotence, omniscience, and omnipresence.

For example, consider the movie *Eye in the Sky* from some years ago. In brief, the movie unfolds around the search for high-profile terrorists who have been tracked to a house in Nairobi, Kenya. The original plan had been to capture the terrorists, but when it becomes clear that a plot is underway to stage a suicide bombing that will kill at least 80 people, then the mission changes to that of attacking the house with a drone-directed bomb. The only hesitation is that an innocent, young 9-year-old girl has set up her stand to sell her family's freshly baked bread to passersby, and her location next to the house means she will also be killed should the house be bombed.

We have been introduced to the lovely little girl and her parents earlier in the film. They are winsome, the portrait of a normal, loving family. And thus, we all are drawn into the drama: Do we bomb the terrorists and risk killing the innocent child as well, or do we spare her but at the expense of letting the terrorists go on with their plot to kill countless others?

We are seared by this human drama while we are also fascinated with the technology that enables the plot to be seen and to draw us in. Here is my reason for inserting this movie in my reflection upon our fascination with technology. The movie cleverly, in a dramatic but realistic way, introduces us to the anguish of the characters who include: the British colonel (Helen Mirren) who pushes for the attack, her commanding general (Alan Rickman) who supports her but listens to other points of view, the drone pilot (Aaron Paul) who hesitates to pull the trigger and asks for a revised risk assessment, and several other governmental and political officials who are consulted and asked to sign off on the mission or not. You can feel for these people when their deep human values and care for life forces them to a breaking point at which some decision must be made, or as the saying goes, when not to decide is to decide, and many lives are potentially at risk.

This cast does a magnificent job bringing us into the horrible process of deciding. But it is not just the human cast that sets up this movie to make it a profound production.

Also revealed to us is the incredible technology that makes all of this possible and frightening.

For example, the camera shifts scenes from the colonel's command post in Sussex to the control room in Whitehall, where her commanding general is sitting around a table with governmental and political leaders, to the pilot's command console in Las Vegas, to the village of Nairobi, Kenya, where an on-the-ground surveillance operative is guiding the very sophisticated cameras. One of these cameras is the size and appearance of a bird positioned outside the house, and another is the size of a beetle able to enter the house directed by the remote control of the operative's smartphone, making possible the eavesdropping on the terrorists putting on suicide vests. And at critical points in the excruciating decision-making process, various other leaders, including the U.S. Secretary of State on a state visit in China, are projected on the screens, enveloping all of the players in a cocoon of visual connectedness that spans more than three continents while the drone flies patiently overhead, waiting for the electronic signal to attack.

It is the technology that weaves this single mission into a tragic drama of life and death to be determined by characters asking themselves, "What is the good in this case?" The actors and those of us watching appear to be insulated in a closed, dark room with a screen that brings us into the most intimate closeness with persons who will live or die based upon the decision that will be made.

This drama of being forced to choose whether others should live or die has always been with us in some form. But now the drama has escalated. In classical theology, the attributes of God were considered to be omnipotence (God is all-powerful), omniscience (God is all-knowing), and omnipresence (God's eye sees all). Technology has now bequeathed to us those attributes.

This is what I am calling the "technocomplex." It is a state of mind caught up in a technological haze, seemingly possessing the god-like attributes of omnipotence, omniscience, and omnipresence. We hold unbelievable power, enough to destroy whole groups of people and the earth itself, but no moral mandate to direct the power; we have access to knowledge and the never-ceasing flow of data, but no consciousness with which to discover its meaning. With our eyes in the sky that formerly belonged to God (see Zechariah 4:10), we can see everything everywhere all of the time, but we lose sight of the fact that we are also being seen and counted simply as one more statistic.

Something is wrong within the technocomplex. The rate of PTSD among drone pilots exceeds 30%. And the destruction of life leaves us with the glassy, empty-eyed stare of the characters in *Eye in the Sky* at the movie's end, a soul-less state in which no matter who wins the war, humanity loses.

MENTAL HEALTH'S
FOUR-LEGGED STOOL

On March 20, 1925, The Rev. Frederick Lewis Donaldson preached a memorable sermon at Westminster Abbey in which he gave a definition of evil:

> *Wealth without work*
> *Pleasure without conscience*
> *Knowledge without character*
> *Commerce without morality*
> *Science without humanity*
> *Worship without sacrifice*
> *Politics without principle*

Donaldson's elegant description of evil reminds me of the interlocking dynamic of evil and mental illness. But we have no reference point with which to consider evil and mental illness unless we understand mental health. And to describe mental health I will use the metaphor of a four-legged stool.

I call it the four-legged stool on which our life rests. If a leg is missing, or if a leg is too short, the stool is not balanced, and we may fall off. The legs are work, play, affection, and spirituality, and this is the way I describe each of the legs.

WORK

It is not true that people do not want to work. It is not true that most people are lazy. Most people want to work. Those who do not want to work quite often are found to be people who have been abused in the workplace through demeaning duties, bullying supervisors, or pay that does not provide means to match the cost of living. In these cases, people "drop out," turn to crime, attempt to con the system for welfare, or drop into a debilitating life of drugs, suicide, or institutionalization.

For example, as reported in the *Proceedings of the National Academy of Sciences*, "The mortality rate for white men and women ages 45–54 with less than a college education took a sharp turn upward in 1999" (November 5, 2015). What has happened to account for this spike in the mysterious deaths of these people?

In the same article, five reasons for the high mortality rate were offered: our nation's opioid epidemic, alcohol poisoning, suicide, the end of the American dream (coinciding with the disappearances of manufacturing and construction jobs), and the breakdown of family support networks.

Underlying all of these proposed reasons is the loss of meaningful, rewarding work, the first leg on our stool of mental health.

PLAY

The second leg of our stool is play. Even though we may not do it well or often enough, we all know we feel better when we play. It is a biological/archetypal force in our lives. When Jung was in his sixties and seventies, he often would sit by the Zurich "sea" and build sand castles, sometimes joined by little kids who wandered by.

Play, when we lose ourselves in it, restores our sanity. New neural pathways are created in our brain. We laugh. We create. We move our bodies in new ways. We find a joy that releases the stress of work and worry, or as Dr. Vanderscharen of Utrecht University puts it, "Dopamine makes us want to play, while endorphins make us enjoy it."

And, if we are mindful about our play, we may even take it back with us to our workplace and approach our work in a new way. "This is the real secret of life," says Alan Watts, "to be completely engaged in what you are doing in the here and now. And instead of calling it work, we realize it is play" (YouTube, April 10, 2019).

AFFECTION

This third leg, affection, is the stuff of poetry, love songs, and Hallmark cards. It is the dynamic in relationships that breaks down walls of misunderstanding, mistrust, and hostility. And it begins in the first moments of life when infants are held lovingly by parents whose adoring eyes connect with their baby's expectant gaze. In that first encounter between mother and child, a secure attachment is formed that enables the developing child to feel secure in all of life, to be able to give and receive love.

"The meeting of two personalities is like the contact of two chemical substances; if there is any reaction, both are transformed" (Jung, 1933, p. 47). This is the epitome of mental health, is it not, to be able to experience this level of affection with another human being (or pet), to feel secure enough to be trustingly vulnerable in acts of friendship, sexuality, and teamwork; while, on the other hand, one is able to recognize those persons, places, and events that are not safe physically, mentally, emotionally, psychologically, or spiritually. In these cases, love compels us to leave others for the sake of our souls.

SPIRITUALITY

Which brings us to the fourth leg, spirituality. It is the experience of Ultimate Concern that connects your deepest self with meaning, purpose, and a moral core that makes possible a healthy relationship with all sentient beings. You may find this experience through participation in organized religion, but you may not. In fact, you may have to escape organized religion in order to realize your authentic spirituality.

If you have found the idea of spirituality to be so vague that you either feel confined or just uncertain what it would look like, you may find helpful the following list of behaviors that describe the spirituality experience:

- Being honest ... and able to see yourself as others see you.
- Being able to stay focused in the present, to be alert, unhurried, and attentive.
- Being able to rest, relax, and create a still, peaceful state of mind.
- Developing a deeper sense of empathy for others.
- Finding the capacity for forgiveness.
- Being able to be with someone who is suffering, while still being hopeful.
- Learning better judgment, for example, about when to speak or act, when not to speak or act, and when to remain silent or do nothing.
- Learning how to give without feeling drained.
- Being able to grieve and let go.
  (The Royal College of Psychiatrists, p. 9)

This is the leg on our four-legged stool that gives meaning and a depth perspective to the legs of work, play, and affection. For if we care nothing for the Ultimate, it is most likely we will have ultimate care for nothing.

CONCLUSION

Sigmund Freud's definition of health is having the capacity to work and to love. I have extended his definition by placing mental health on the four-legged stool of work, play, affection, and spirituality. In so doing, I hope I have extended our range of consideration for what a mentally healthy person might look like. In this season of bizarre and dangerous politics, we do well to review Donaldson's definition of evil. But even more closely to our everyday life, we must consider the mental health not only of ourselves but of those entrusted with our welfare as it is experienced in work, play, affection, and spirituality.

THE MEANING OF HEALTH AND THE HEALTH OF MEANING

On January 14, 1960, Paul Tillich presented a paper to the New York Society of Clinical Psychiatry entitled "The Meaning of Health." Dr. Tillich, at that time a professor at Harvard Divinity School, had established a reputation as a philosopher/theologian who recognized the inseparable tie that held together the disciplines of theology, medicine, and psychology. What made his insights so profound was his capacity to consider not only the roles of those disciplines in their respective clinical settings but also their roles in society as a whole, where the disease of individuals impacts the well-being of families, groups, and even nations. As a refugee himself from Hitler's Germany, Tillich had seen first-hand how the insanity of persons infected the nation, leading to the establishment of the Third Reich and Germany's eventual collapse in World War II.

As was characteristic of Tillich's well-researched papers, this one on the meaning of health was elegant, deep, and profound in its far-reaching orbit of elements affecting the health of persons and societies. During the street theatrics of what passed for political deliberations in Congress and the White House at the time of my writing this past week, I thought about Tillich's paper, the very different age in which he wrote it, and the conditions making health care a crisis in our country.

I will come back to Tillich's discussion in a moment, but first I want to say more about the different conditions separating our present time from the years in which Tillich lived. What comes to my mind immediately are the conversations I have with physicians in my consulting room. As a whole, they talk about their disenchantment with medicine. They reference many things, most of which are visible to the public:

- the aggressive drive for profits, controlled by management gurus who take the temperature of the markets as more important than the well-being of their patients;
- the awesome developments of medical technology, making possible diagnostic and treatment options not even dreamed about during Tillich's lifetime;
- the astronomical costs of these technologies, making it almost impossible for the survival of small practices while fueling the absurd growth of our medical complexes and corporations;

- the alliance of the pharmaceutical industry
  with the individuals and medical institutions
  that further dehumanize the patients who have
  become conditioned in our drug-obsessed society
  to take whatever makes them feel good, especially
  if it has the blessing of a doctor still carrying some
  remnant of the hallowed regard once ascribed to
  the medical profession;
- the role of the insurance companies in dictating
  (a) the appropriate treatment for a medical
  condition, and (b) the method and duration
  of the treatment, as well as (c) the medications
  recommended;
- the numberless forms of new age treatments
  marketed in competition with traditional
  medical care, boastful of their curative powers,
  in competition with the triadic monopoly of
  medical conglomeration, pharmaceutical giants,
  and insurance authorities;
- the loss of jobs, lifestyles, homes, and old
  neighborhoods where the factories and businesses
  shut down either because the old products no
  longer are used, they can be produced more
  economically, or new technologies make the old
  work lines obsolete in our emerging technocratic
  world where one robot can replace five human
  beings, or where one technician in a small office

thousands of miles away can perform the tasks formerly requiring a room full of people.

In all of these examples of changes over the past 40 years, each one has a profound impact upon our understanding of "the meaning of health *and* the health of meaning." The implications are quite apparent in those examples having to do with the medical profession but perhaps less obvious in my last example. But it is in that last example—the loss of jobs, lifestyles, homes, neighborhoods—where a very scary thing is happening that affects the health of each of us while also offering us a deeper look into the meaning of health.

That scary thing is the loss of meaning. It should frighten each of us that the 2016 report from the National Center for Health Studies shows a sharp increase in the U.S. death rate of younger and middle-age white men. These surprising and disturbing statistics prompted an all-out study to find the possible causes. Here are the results: suicides, drug-related poisonings, heavy alcohol abuse, and drug overdoses.

But the important question is, What accounts for the unexpected spike in these deaths? And for that answer, we do not need the analyses of our sociologists. All we must do is to reflect upon the misery of those places and persons who have lost all meaning in their lives. There is no purpose, no hope of there ever being one again, and—ultimately—this results in the loss of meaning, a terminal disease of the soul.

Hold that thought while I return briefly to a summary of Tillich's paper. Speaking to the New York Society of Clinical Psychiatry, he attempted to provide an overview describing a way to consider the meaning of health. To do this, Tillich drew upon his philosophical and theological background that understood human nature as a unified whole of many dimensions. There are several dimensions to human existence that may be described as:

1. the *mechanical*—referring to the body parts such as the skeletal system that supports the physical structure of the human body;

2. the *biological*—having to do with organs, tissues, and interrelated processes that make possible life itself;

3. the *chemical*—dealing with the interworking of those biological processes, as we descend into the deeper complexities of the biological organism;

4. the *historical*—referencing a term from the social sciences to describe the role of societies, groups, and organizations and how they impact persons for better or worse, health or disease;

5. the *spiritual*—encompassing all the other dimensions with a safety net for meaning-gathering, purposive-serving, hope-generating

functions that make possible what Joseph Campbell has referred to as "the joyful participation in the sorrows of the world," a soulful embrace of the cosmos with a trusting affirmation of that "something" that is alive in each of us and connects us with the wonder and awe of the universe.

Without this meaning, our souls die, and with it our hopes and dreams, our societies, our civilization. Without recognition of the importance of each person having access to the conditions that make such meaning possible, then there can be no vision for a "health plan" that is anything more than a political ploy, a self-serving subterfuge that destroys the meaning of health because there is no health of meaning.

GUERNICA IN A WORLD
WITH NO MORAL CENTER

Guernica is a town located in the province of Biscay, within the Autonomous Community of the Basque Country, Spain. Today, the town claims a population between 16,000 and 17,000 residents, symbolized by the Tree, an oak that represents the Basque people and their history. Also, standing with a view toward the Tree is a Monument to Peace, commissioned to commemorate the terrorizing bombing of the town on April 26, 1937, when Hitler's Luftwaffe killed 1,654 civilians and razed the town. In one of his greatest works, Picasso catches the horror of that massacre of civilians in his painting "Guernica."

In the absence of any visual image, I am going to turn to the PBS "Treasures of the World" verbal narrative of what happened to the people of Guernica on that day in April 1937, when children, women, and men went excitedly to visit with each other, socializing innocently in the town's marketplace.

It was market day when the church bells of Santa Maria sounded the alarm that afternoon in 1937. People from the surrounding hillside crowded the town square.

"Every Monday was a fair in Guernica," says Jose Monastery, eyewitness to the bombing. "They attacked when there were a lot of people there. And they knew when their bombing would kill the most. When there are more people, more people would die."

For over three hours, twenty-five or more of Germany's best-equipped bombers, accompanied by at least twenty more Messerschmitt and Fiat fighters, dumped one hundred thousand pounds of high-explosive incendiary bombs on the village, slowly and systematically pounding it to rubble.

"We were hiding in the shelters and praying. I only thought of running away. I was so scared. I didn't think about my parents, mother, house, nothing. Just escape. Because during those three and one-half hours, I thought I was going to die."
(Luis Aurtonetrea, eyewitness)

Those trying to escape were cut down by the strafing machine guns of fighter planes. "They keep going back and forth, sometimes in a long line, sometimes in close formation. It was as if they were practicing

82

new moves. They must have fired thousands of
bullets." (Juan Guezureya, eyewitness)

The fires that engulfed the city burned for three
days. Seventy percent of the city was destroyed.
Sixteen hundred civilians—one third of the
population—were killed or wounded.

This would not be the last time in World War II when a city was destroyed and civilians were murdered. Dresden comes to mind when between 35,000 and 135,000 people died during the Allied bombing, February 13–14, 1945. Also coming to mind are Hiroshima with the loss of 90,000 to 146,000 people and Nagasaki with 39,000 to 80,000 people killed during bombings of August 6 and 9, 1945.

But, to return to Guernica, it was Picasso's painting that brings home to us the continued terrifying images of animals (the bull, the horse, and the dove), people (the devastated woman cradling in her arms a lifeless child, the dismembered soldier), and objects (the horseshoe, the strangely appearing lamp, tongues shaped like knives, and the disturbingly chilling image of an eye or light bulb that looks down on the macabre devastation).

In addition, something further disturbs us about the slaughtering of people and a village like Guernica. It is this: Guernica had no strategic value as a military target! (See the PBS conclusion on the matter as well.) In other words, innocent people died, animals were brutalized, and a town was devastated by military tactics that served only as a practice run to perfect the technique of attacking civilian populations in order to terrorize the world and further the military goals of Franco, Hitler, Mussolini, and others in the war machine of the so-called Axis powers.

Observe how three forces came together in planning and executing the attack on Guernica. These forces were: (1) a fascination with technology, and in particular the technology that could be applied to warfare; (2) the obsession with power and the danger of being taken over or possessed with a power complex, personal or collective; and (3) how this fascination with technology in the hands of a despotic ruler and nation with no conscious moral center may explode in a frenzy of nationalism, imperialism, militarism, and the hubris of disregard for boundaries and the well-being of neighbors.

Sound familiar? It should. And the most frightening prospect is that this may occur so slowly, so far removed from the basic concerns of our everyday life, that the danger is obscured until it is too late to head it off. Like an infection in the body that must be diagnosed at its early onset, so do we need to be attentive to the interpretation given for events in our social and political life.

For example, are we oblivious to the fact that children may be separated from their parents at our borders? That children may be placed in cages without proper clothes and hygiene for indefinite periods of time? That a father and his daughter risked their lives crossing a river where they drowned seeking hope in a world where hope has long been out of reach for thousands of people?

Considering our political controversies on the topic of immigration, is the problem that we need to erect walls and barriers to prevent people from crossing our borders? Or might it be the case that we are not understanding and addressing the causes that lead people to risk everything, even their lives, to find safety, security, and a possible promising future for themselves and their children?

Are we oblivious to these considerations? I think not. Returning to the memory of Guernica, as I mentioned earlier, the three forces that intersected leading to the attack on that village were conditions that are capable of appearing in our time: a fascination with technology and its application for making war; a drive for power with such an obsession that it became a power complex driving the corrupting governments of General Franco, Hitler, and Mussolini, leaders of the Axial powers; and the absence of consciousness of a moral center within those individuals whose leadership made possible the monstrous attack on Guernica.

Whether or not the tragic episode of history repeats itself depends upon our consciousness and our intention to see that Guernica does not occur while we placidly stroll through the marketplace of our high-tech village, fascinated with our iPhones, enjoying a bull market that could become the bull of Picasso's "Guernica."

CHAPTER THREE

MENTAL HEALTH

The privilege of a lifetime is to become who you truly are.
—C. G. Jung

BEGINNINGS AND ENDINGS

Two pictures linger strongly in my mind as I turn to leave summer and enter the fall season, which has slipped up on me quite unexpectedly—again.

The first picture is of our granddaughter standing triumphantly on her front steps just before leaving for her first day in first grade. All the preparations have taken place: new clothes, a new book bag, and countless conversations about what to expect the first day of this most auspicious occasion. She stands holding Miller, her tuxedo cat, in her arms, just before kissing him goodbye, and just before symbolically closing the door on her early childhood that was so very brief for all of us who delighted in sharing her emerging spirit, curiosity, and sense of wonder these past six years.

The second picture is of my wife's aging parents. Now in their eighties, life is collapsing around them, confining him to an Alzheimer's ward and she to an assisted care community that supports her precarious faltering movement with her ever-present walker. You see in their eyes the familiar memories receding and escaping their reach, leaving embarrassing lacunae in their conversations.

Strange. I feel somewhat disoriented as I place myself between these two pictures. This is what it is like, I think, "to be at sea" and caught in the turbulence that occurs when two strong currents intersect, when the day is drearily foggy with strong, chilling winds and cascading waves.

Psychologically, it is to be caught between the two very powerful opposites of a beginning and an ending. But I know also that in the back of my mind there is still a force trying to bubble up. That force is the symbolic meaning of these images I see in the pictures.

Each picture represents a symbolic image that reaches ancient and universal depths in us. Knowledge of those depths may be used both for understanding and serving one another, but also for exploiting each other politically, economically, and militarily.

For example, take the phrase "morning in America." It suggests a beginning, hope, promise, maybe even an advantageous moment in national life that already has passed by other nations, but not America. Those associations so evocative of quite strong emotions may be employed for good or bad. They may be used for political gain and destructive ends, or for the marshaling of efforts for the benefit and well-being of all. All of that is to say that the archetypal image of a "beginning" has the capacity to unleash great energy that may be destructive or beneficial depending upon the "coloration" it is given.

In the same way, at the other end of this spectrum of opposites, the image of an "ending" also has the potential to animate people in bizarre ways. Consider, for example, the image of "ending" as it is conveyed by current preoccupations with "the end of the world."

The archetype can be traced back to our human origins, as all the world's religions have some variation of this notion of an ending for all things. But there are periods in human history when an image of the end of the world erupts with volcanic power and seizes the minds of people. I think we are living in one such time, witnessed by widespread references to the ancient Mayan calendar that supposedly projects the end of the world in December 2012; interpretations of some prophecies by Nostradamus thought to name 2012 as an end time; blogs, books, and the establishing of particular communities in preparation for civilization's collapse and/or the extinction of the planet; and the best-selling *Left Behind* series of books that predicts a rapture in which true believers will be taken up to heaven before the imminent destruction of the world by God, at a date sometime specifically named by many other religious fundamentalist groups.

Enough of these examples, I hope, point out how an archetypal image can seize the minds of groups of people with unforeseen consequences economically, politically, and socially. To return to my earlier metaphor, this is what happens to us psychologically when we experience ourselves being "at sea," caught in the turbulence of forces acting on us and all around us.

And so, you may wonder, how have I dealt with the turbulence felt in the crosscurrents of my two pictures? Let me describe it most briefly like this. When I face my thoughts and feelings, when I do not ignore them or let my attention be diverted, when I get disentangled from the thoughts and feelings, the turbulence clears. It is then not so much that the feelings and thoughts and images have me under their control, but rather that I have them.

The pictures are the same and my feelings are the same, but I am different.

CHRISTMAS
AND HUMAN NATURE

"Christmas" is all around me. How can it not be, since the holiday that bears the name of Christmas unleashes a euphoric shopping extravaganza unlike anything the world has known before—at least in the form of commercial exploitation.

But, again, when we consider human nature, why would we be surprised at this crass manipulation of our deepest fears, needs, and yearnings. I am referring here to our fear of darkness and what it constellates within us, foremost of which is the archetypal yearning for light. Watching the darkness gather around us on this shortest day of the year, sensing the chill of the winter solstice, I marvel once more at the profound relationship between the holiday "season" and the season of our winter solstice here in the northern hemisphere.

Which brings me to this observation: It is the nature of human beings to fear darkness, to seek light, to study our relationship to the sun, moon, and stars, and to struggle with the many facets of our finitude. These include anxiety around the uncertainties of life and death, a great grief over the loss of those dear to us, a tragic sense of guilt in the knowledge of how we have hurt and betrayed others, a competitiveness for resources, the fear and distrust of strangers, as well as an aggression that can become barbaric.

All of these aspects of human nature shade toward the somber, grave side of our existence. But, as you are already thinking, there is of course another side that affirms life in its darkness even before the light appears. These qualities of life include an innate sense of wonder and empathy; a capacity to love, to make friends, and to give and receive gifts; and the ability to forgive. They include the capacity to sing, dance, and make merry even in the darkest times; to seek and follow a moral code; to strive for justice while also granting mercy; to express our affirmation of life in great works of art, literature, music, architecture, scientific endeavors, health, and education; to display kindness toward all animals and the earth; as well as a desire to extend our human family into the future and out into the cosmos with an intuitive sense that there is more awaiting us than meets the eye.

This also is human nature—the buoyant side marked with resilience and lightness of spirit. These qualities as well as those listed previously describe the mountains and valleys of our basic being as humans. Like the seasons of our existence on the planet earth we call home, these qualities move between light and darkness, warmth and chill, verdancy and decay, life and death.

And it is quite likely that the time of our winter solstice is the time historically and existentially that we ponder these qualities with ultimate concern: Will we make it through this long night, and will we ever again experience new life?

The ultimate concern evoked by these qualities, traits, and questions defines us as human beings. This ultimate concern arises inevitably in each of us, and because of that we add this most important fact to the description of human nature: Human beings are by nature religious.

It is this religious attitude, not just a dogma or creed, that ushers in our Christmas celebrations. In the spirit of that religious attitude, Jerry Herman, the remarkable musician and lyricist, created his song, "We Need a Little Christmas."

Haul out the holly,
Put up the tree before my spirit falls again;
Fill up the stockings,
I may be rushing things but deck the halls again
now.
For we need a little Christmas,
Right this very minute,
Candles in the window,
Carols at the spinet,
Yes, we need a little Christmas,
Right this very minute,

It hasn't snowed a single flurry,
But Santa, dear, we're in a hurry.
So climb down the chimney,
Turn on the brightest of lights I've ever seen.
Slice up the fruitcake;
It's time we hung some tinsel on that evergreen
bough.
For I've grown a little leaner,
Grown a little colder,
Grown a little sadder,
Grown a little older.
And I need a little angel,
Sitting on my shoulder.
I need a little Christmas now!
For we need a little music,
Need a little laughter,
Need a little singing,
Ringing through the rafter.
And we need a little snappy
"Happy ever after."
We need a little Christmas now!

Herman wrote this song for the 1966 Broadway production of *Mame*, starring Angela Lansbury. The Christmas song comes unexpectedly in the story line when the bohemian, carefree Mame loses her fortune in the Wall Street crash of 1929, leaving her destitute in her own psychological winter solstice with the additional surprise of having to provide for her young nephew, Patrick, because of the news that her brother has died.

So what does Mame do? She sings and dances her way through the darkness in the best spirit of Christmas, revealing a most-unexpected Christ figure through her unconditional love for Patrick, her loyalty to her old staff, and her unfading affirmation of life. And along the way, she prompts others to celebrate her own infectious joy to the world!

Mame's celebration of Christmas is also part of our human nature. Granted, it can be exploited by the call of the hucksters in our marketplaces. That is true. But it is also true that the human spirit winks at these diversions, and at the end of the day looks toward the stars with wonder, hope, joy, compassion for others, and a deep longing for peace.

FROM HEART TO HEART: REFLECTIONS DURING MEMORIAL DAY

Here is a true story. Outside my office is a balcony accessible by steps frequented not only by humans who come to my office, but also by various friendly animals who drop by for a visit or to see if there might be any food or water in the small dishes outside my door. Don't worry. The food supply is not to encourage feral activity but to assist in occasional emergency support until, ideally, the critters can move along and find, or be assisted in finding, permanent homes.

One of the visitors I observed was a black cat I named "Ninja" because he would slip by only rarely and very unobtrusively, staying out of sight as best he could.

Only, Ninja was not a "he" but a "she," apparently, because after a long absence she appeared one morning with a little kitten that had a tortoise-shelled coloring that was arrestingly striking had it not been for the malnourished state of its little body as well as that of Ninja's.

I filled the two little bowls with food and water, went back inside my waiting room, and observed the mother and her kitten from a window. The first thing that struck me was how the mother did not run off and out of sight but remained close by as I put food and water in the dishes. Then a fascinating little drama took place. "Ninja" walked over to the dishes and showed the kitten what to do, nibbling briefly at the food and sipping quickly at the water before backing away while her kitten ate.

The mother cat lay down three feet or so from the dishes and quietly observed the feeding kitten. Not once did Ninja show any impatience. Only after the kitten had obviously finished its meal and come over to begin play with her mother did Ninja get up and feed herself. Finally, both apparently satisfied, the mother guided her playful kitten across the balcony and back down the stairs.

What struck me so strongly in that brief episode was the nurturing, unselfish behavior of this feral and very hungry mother cat. It reminded me of a study conducted in 1964 and reported in the *American Journal of Psychiatry*. As the research team reported their findings, a group of rhesus monkeys were observed coping with a dilemma set up for a controlled experiment to observe whether or not the monkeys would show a capacity for empathy toward one another.

In the experiment, certain monkeys could feed themselves by pulling on a chain that would deliver food within their reach. However, as the feeding monkeys soon observed, each time they pulled the chain, it delivered a shock to a companion rhesus monkey in another location. Under those conditions, the feeding monkeys elected not to pull the chain and harm others, starving themselves, in one case, up to 12 days.

Experiments such as this one and the careful study of various primates in their native habitats have demonstrated a surprising capacity for, and practice of, empathy within the animal kingdom. Through the disciplines of biology, neurology, psychiatry, psychology, ethology, anthropology, and others, we add clearly to our insights about the place of compassion not only among humans but within and among all primates as well.

The result? Let me state it most succinctly: We are "hard-wired" for compassion. It is only a partial understanding of all primates, including humans, that focuses on aggression, violence, and selfishness. True, those qualities mark our history to a disturbing degree, but our human evolution and survival have depended upon acts of love and compassion as well. Strangely, only now are we beginning to re-evaluate those qualities on the positive side of the ledger that enable us not only to prevail but to find meaning, inspiration, and joy in life—even in our darkest moments.

For instance, consider the life and late work of the German pianist and composer Ludwig van Beethoven (1770–1827). By age 30, he had already arrived at a pinnacle of achievement for a musician, recognized as one of the outstanding pianists and composers in his day with the promise of historical prominence. But he was a miserable man who reported to his brother that he had considered ending his life.

He was going deaf. It was a medical condition that threatened, and eventually resulted in, the permanent total loss of his hearing. But truth be known, he was by all reports a pretty miserable man before his approaching deafness. He was eccentric, explosive, contentious, and self-preoccupied. Pity the poor waiter in the Vienna restaurant who might bring Beethoven a dish not acceptable for whatever reason and have it thrown back in the waiter's face!

But, to grant some allowances to the famous composer, we also must remember the overwhelming external stress of those years of his life. They were filled not only with the personal vexations of living alone and trying to make a living as a musician but also having to contend with family tragedies and a war brought home to Vienna by the invading armies of Napoleon, whose canons tested the last resolve of Beethoven's hearing and whose occupying armies brought the horror of war to the streets and cafes of the musician's everyday life.

My point of focusing on Beethoven in the context of considering the role of love and empathy in human existence is for the following reason. It seems to me that he found something in the human soul during those last years of deafness and warring violence that demonstrates the case I am trying to make.

During that last decade of Beethoven's life, he composed some of his most complex and inspiring works. These include not only string quartets and piano sonatas, but also the profound *Missa Solemnis,* which is often overlooked and under-performed, and the Ninth Symphony, which cannot be overlooked and has not been under-performed!

In these works, Beethoven finds an "ode to joy" (Ninth Symphony) but also an "inner and outer peace"—words and music he "hears" that offer an understanding of human potential in the face of life's uncertainties and tragedies. To return to my opening paragraphs, in which I suggested that in primates there is a "hard-wiring" for empathy, I am suggesting further that we can trace that fundamental and universal trait as it appears in human suffering. Love and empathy form our basic nature and connect all human beings in a shared melody that arises from our hearts with joy, hope, and yearning for peace.

At the top of Beethoven's score for the *Missa Solemnis,* he wrote, "From the Heart—May it Return to the Heart." The piece concludes with the words, *Dona nobis pacem*—grant us peace.

TO THE MEMORY OF A VANISHING WORLD

Sometime in 1953, Carl and Emma Jung were preparing for dinner, and Carl was rummaging around to find a bottle of wine for the occasion. Finally, he found just the right bottle, a 45-year-old bottle of Bordeaux. But when they settled in and prepared for a toast with that vintage wine, Carl and Emma could not find words to capture their thoughts and feelings. Finally, Carl managed the very poignant toast with which I have entitled this blog: "To the memory of a vanishing world."

Dierdre Bair tells this story in her very thorough biography of Jung. In her account of the Jungs in 1953, Bair describes them as frail. Carl would have been 78 at the time; Emma was 71, but her health had seriously deteriorated with cancer as early as 1952. Neither had long to live, and already they had lost many of their closest friends.

The poignancy of that moment when they tipped their glasses with Carl's toast is not lost on many of us, especially those in the last half of our lives. Truth be known, by the time we reach the mid-point of life, say around age 35, we have seen many worlds vanish. How can we not recognize at least some truth in the Buddhist idea of the impermanence of all things: All that rises falls away. So it is with our personal lives, and so it is with our physical, social, family, and political worlds.

And yet, could we not say, that some "worlds" fall away more strikingly than others, depending upon the time and circumstances that frame a "world?" For example, consider how the technology of our present time makes everything appear to go faster. We don't simply want just any connection to the internet; we want the service that will connect us faster—perhaps spontaneously! This technology today has so impacted our lives that we spend an inordinate amount of time trying to read the manuals supposedly describing how to power up the gadgets that then rule our lives.

The fact that I do not stay ahead of this wave of technological advances was brought home to me in a very dramatic way recently. I had just concluded a therapy session with a young woman who is chief finance officer with an investment group. She fumbled through her purse, obviously becoming more and more frustrated trying to locate her checkbook. Having finally located it, she looked up at me while writing the check and said, "You know, you really are archaic. You're the only person I write checks for anymore!"

I don't think she meant to say anything harmful or with a hostile intent. Her comment was simply a fact that came to her mind describing something very peculiar in her world. In her world, checks are obsolete, and people who conduct business dependent upon checking, well, those people are "archaic." They belong to a vanishing world.

What she said is true—at least part of it. I know I am not archaic, but I also realize that checks will soon be a thing of the past as more and more banking and financial exchanges are done online. In fact, even now the business of printing checks has taken a significant downturn.

So now it's ebooks, Facebook, Twitter, smartphones, and iPads that do unbelievable things through their apps. And I have to confess that when I walk inside our local Apple store, I feel an excitement that is very hard to describe. It is, I believe, the thrill that we experience anytime we create something, or when we discover anything new that astonishes us.

To say this yet another way, I think it is the feeling that must have come to all explorers of unknown worlds. Imagine what it is like to step on the surface of a previously unexplored continent, or island, or object floating in space! Something in each of us delights in that adventure because it is an adventure of the spirit. Walter Isaacson quotes Steve Jobs's grand realization that the task of his Apple company was the creation of possibilities people had never dreamed of but that have the potential to evoke wonder and enhance life. Think, for example, of the ways in which iPads are making possible new ways of communicating for people with autism.

Think of that new world coming into being as the old world vanishes.

And think of many more possibilities before us as this new world emerges! Yes, some of these are very scary, but many of them offer a deeper sanity with avenues for communicating, tools for healing, enticements for educating, handles for lifting ourselves out of poverty and prejudice, as well as structures for creating an environment that will inspire us with new prospects for working, living, and building a planetary culture.

This seems to be our fate, as it has always been, to live this moment between the vanishing world and the emerging world. What may be different about our particular time is this: We are markedly self-conscious of our moment, largely due to the ever-present images projected by the media. Second, this self-consciousness is without borders. Lastly, the stakes are very high as the well-being of each of us, and our earth, depends upon how we respond to these emerging new possibilities.

So, yes, I agree with the woman who described me as archaic, belonging to the vanishing world. I am that, but I am also an aspirant who cheers for the possibilities of our emerging world. Can we not be both?

I think here of how T. S. Eliot concluded his "East Coker":

Home is where one starts from. As we grow older
The world becomes stranger, the pattern more
complicated
Of dead and living. Not the intense moment
Isolated, with no before and after,
But a lifetime burning in every moment
And not the lifetime of one man only
But of old stones that cannot be deciphered.
There is a time for the evening under starlight,
A time for the evening under lamplight
(The evening with the photograph album).
Love is most nearly itself
When here and now cease to matter.
Old men out to be explorers
Here and now does not matter
We must be still and still moving
Into another intensity
For a further union, a deeper communion
Through the dark cold and the empty desolation,
The wave cry, the wind cry, the vast waters
Of the petrel and the porpoise.
In my end is my beginning.

WHY REASON
ALSO NEEDS A VACATION

Well, it's that time of year again. If you have not yet had your vacation, you probably are way overdue and plan to take one very soon—I hope. That is, unless you are trapped in that mindset, all too familiar here in these United States, where workaholism is associated with patriotism, machismo, true capitalism, the opposite of laziness, religious piety, duty, and so forth. All of these things oil the years of productivity and are driven by the obsession that profits must increase and that development knows no bounds! Incredible!

But it is prevalent. No wonder we have suicides, divorces, mental illnesses, and violence. No wonder that most people I see in my consulting room confess that they are miserable. No wonder one ideal that keeps surfacing in the fantasies of people is either to escape to the country and get away from it all, or to work even harder so as to arrive at the supreme goal of being able to sit back, play golf, and "manage their wealth." Incredible that "managing wealth" replaces baseball as the national pastime. The infrastructures crumble, habitats are destroyed, neighborhoods are ravaged, schools lack resources, religious wars threaten civilization, and we "manage our wealth." Incredible!

But wait, this is not about that madness. In fact, this is about something entirely different. This is about "vacation," particularly the vacation of reason. Why this topic? Because the people I counsel are notably physically exhausted; more than anything, they are mentally exhausted. They have exhausted their "critical reasoning."

Think about it. Remember that vacation you enjoyed so much, or the one you wanted to enjoy but never gave yourself the opportunity to go for it? I am talking about that time at the beach: a sunny day, a nice shady umbrella, a soft breeze, no worries about the work back home, perhaps some easy beach music in the background, the sound of surf, and—here it comes—that novel you waited to read! It may not have been one of the world's great classics of memorable literature, but it captured your attention. You could hardly put it down. When you did finish it, you felt refreshed, inspired, renewed in some way. You just enjoyed a mental vacation! Now you can get back to the grind. Somehow you have found your old energy, your old zip. You see the old stuff in new ways with new solutions and exciting outcomes. Or, you may throw it all aside and find the courage, ways, and means to do what you always have wanted to do.

My friend, a college professor who works very hard preparing for his classes, lecturing, researching, grading papers, counseling students, and tending to administrative duties, never allows himself to read fiction. A waste of time! Or, at best, an indulgence that would interrupt his path toward full professorship! But then he peeped inside the first volume of the *Harry Potter* eight-volume set and has not been able to stop. He is now finishing volume eight, *The Rise of the Dark Prince,* and feels "somehow refreshed." Incredible!

But not. Actually, he is using another kind of reason. In his daily work, my friend employs his critical reason, but in this reading of fiction he follows the lead of another kind of reason, one I call heart-reason.

I am indebted, in part to Blaise Pascal, of course, who expressed it best like this:

> *The heart has reasons which reason knows nothing of . . . We know the truth not only by the reason but by the heart. (Thoughts, #423)*

This is not a reasoning of sentimentality, but a form of reason that is not boxed-in by critical analysis, although it is yet rational. The heart's "reason" is not commandeered by rationalism but rather by a rational process of valuing (as Jung might describe in his typological discussion of "feeling").

And this reason of the heart is influenced by the promptings of the unconscious. Listen to Jung:

As a matter of fact, day after day we live far
beyond the bounds of our consciousness; without
our knowledge, the life of the unconscious is also
going on within us. The more the critical reason
dominates, the more impoverished life becomes; but
the more of the unconscious, and the more of myth
we are capable of making conscious, the more of
life we integrate. Overvalued reason has this in
common with political absolutism: under its
dominion the individual is pauperized.
(MDR, p. 302)

So, yes, take your critical reason on vacation. But let it snooze in the sun while your heart frolics in the surf—and in the novel that has been calling out to you for some time now.

THE SYNDROME OF ESTRANGEMENT:
ANXIETY, ALIENATION, ANGER AND THE DYNAMICS OF EVIL

Something is wrong with us and within us. Something is wrong with the times in which we are living. We may deny it or ignore it with the aid of those 10,000 distractions that cram the habitat in which we work, play, vacation, worship, exercise, govern, and build our homes that are inflated with "entertainment centers."

One rationalization we use to deny the impact of what is happening to us now is to rely on the weak realization that sufferings and injustices are always present in each age. So what is the big deal about our time? What is the "wrong" I am talking about that is any different from other times and places?

Let me try to describe it like this. We may use the metaphors of "the perfect storm" or "critical mass." But I am going to call it a "syndrome," meaning "a group of signs and symptoms that occur together and characterize a particular abnormality or condition" (*Merriam-Webster*). Speaking psychologically, we could also call it a "collective complex," meaning a cluster of images and ideas held together by a strong emotion that is capable of disrupting our conscious life and possessing individuals and groups, leading to irrational thought and behavior that may turn bizarre and destructive. Out of this condition come the most extreme ideologies, religious beliefs, political movements, and idiosyncratic expressions—any of which may pass as reasonable and justifiable during the time of possession.

So, with that description of a syndrome or collective complex, I turn to what has "possessed" us today. I call it "the syndrome of estrangement." This experience of estrangement thrives on its internal organs of anxiety, alienation, and anger, which together lead to a state of psychic possession and the defense mechanism of projection.

I will briefly describe each of these.

Anxiety. Unlike fear, which has a specific focus, anxiety is a condition of unseen stress that leads us to worry, dread, mistrust, and harbor a dark sense of foreboding. Anxiety causes deep suffering because we do not know ways to alleviate the suffering. We cannot "get our minds around it"; we cannot imagine what relief would look like. As I will describe later, the anxiety may be due to a foreboding sense of overwhelm. Whatever it is bothering us is too large, too great for us to be able to hold it, and in fact we may dread the prospect so much that we do not face whatever may be lurking or lunging toward us.

Consider, for example, the phenomena of global warming. The prospects of natural habitats destroyed, ocean-front cities flooded, the onslaught of tens of thousands of refugees seeking higher ground, and the destruction of countless species—these potential scenarios that threaten our planet also threaten our sense of familiarity and safety in a world we thought we would treasure forever. And it is altogether likely that underneath our anxiety over the climate change is a much deeper anxiety concerning the growing awareness of finite resources, to say nothing about the finitude and vulnerability of planet earth itself.

Alienation. Alienation is a state of separation from people, groups, institutions, and/or objects. We think of descriptions such as breach, turning away, breaking off, disaffection, and rupture. This last word, rupture, catches not only the state of affairs but also the mood in which some kind of betrayal has been experienced, severing ties of commitments.

Ruptured—this describes so well our broken relationships in spheres of life we had come to trust and depend upon. In the past 10 to 20 years, we have suffered broken trust with many if not most of our banks, our government, our medical facilities, our religious groups, our politicians, our educational institutions, and our corporations. Worse perhaps even still are the ruptures between family members and old friends as all of us have been drawn into the political polarizations championed by the "talking heads" of radio and television and the money-devouring televangelists of fundamentalist megachurches.

Anger. As I teach people who visit me in my consulting room, anger is a secondary emotion. It seems to be primary because of its raw intensity. But it is secondary because it always follows the experience of some kind of pain: a physical blow, a psychological slight or put-down, a religious assault, an act of betrayal, a great disappointment, an event that overwhelms. Granted, in those cases where the anger turns inward, we become depressed, but otherwise we have been created to protect ourselves when we have been hurt by experiencing the arousal of the autonomic nervous system that prepares us to fight or to flee. Hopefully, where one is nurtured by psychological and spiritual health, the anger is modulated and directed toward peaceful resolution of conflict.

But in certain cases, peaceful resolution is not possible because the state of mind is one of possession. I will describe this more fully later, but now I want only to reference the anger that has seized the world because of our deep anxiety and alienation. All that I described above taxes our autonomic nervous system. The sympathetic sub-system that alerts us to danger needs time and safety to return to a normal baseline level of arousal where the parasympathetic sub-system can operate and support us within the state of mind in which we think clearly and feel with openness the rich vastness of our being, rather than to be trapped within the emotions of terror, hate, envy, resentment, and overwhelm.

Possession. This last state of being when we become trapped within a syndrome or collective complex may be referred to as a state of possession. In such a state, I "am not myself." I cannot think or feel as I normally would. I act and feel as if I am someone else; I am dominated and controlled by some mood or spirit.

For example, the "spirit" of estrangement within the syndrome I have been describing is made up of a psychic whirlwind of anxiety, alienation, and anger. One's mind is clouded by this mental and emotional experience that entraps the person who then regresses to a more primitive level of human functioning, marked by mistrust and aggression. It is here that our demonic self emerges. By demonic self I mean the mood and state of mind arising from the chthonic depths of our personality, bathed in the blood of human conquest and domination.

Projection. But rather than look within at one's own demonic self, it is projected upon some other person or group. The discomfort one feels, the difficulty one experiences, or the impasse one has reached may bring that person to the point of blaming others rather than facing the more difficult task of looking within or looking together at the stymied state of conflict.

And when one's own shadow side is projected upon another person, that individual may be seen as the devil himself. This projection upon others may be used to justify the acts of evil by which persons are demonized and dehumanized with murderess acts of cruelty.

Thus is evil turned loose in the world. Such is the sad state of estrangement in our world today, fragmented and polarized by anxiety, alienation, and anger.

THE REGRESSION OF THE AMERICAN MIND
OR, THE DIS-EASE OF OUR TIME

On a cold, wintry morning, January 20, 1961, during the bleak months and years of an oppressive Cold War with the Soviet Union, John F. Kennedy said in his inauguration speech:

> *And so, my fellow Americans: Ask not what your*
> *country can do for you, ask what you can do for*
> *your country. My fellow citizens of the world:*
> *ask not what America will do for you, but what*
> *together we can do for the freedom of man. Finally,*
> *whether you are citizens of America or citizens of*
> *the world, ask of us here the same high standards of*
> *strength and sacrifice which we ask of you. With a*
> *good conscious our only sure reward, with history*
> *the final judge of our deeds, let us go forth to lead*
> *the land we love, asking His blessings and His*

*help, but knowing that here on earth God's work
must truly be our own.*

Noble words! A clear and sane call to a world order for the benefit of all in very troubled times! But if you Google this inauguration speech and look at the comments that follow, you will be sickened by the cynicism, the shallowness, the stupidity and/or insanity of the people who deride Kennedy's call to the highest of our human nature.

We have traded in the good angels' offering of a vision for a better world and bargained for the cunning apocalypse of the devil, offered with a grand bravado that fuels our lowest nature. What has happened to us? How have we regressed so demonstrably and dramatically that we now:

- Cheer the rattling of our militaristic sabers;
- Applaud the building of a wall that will isolate us from others;
- Tolerate the misogynistic belittling of women as sexual objects inferior to the machismo male;
- Allow a prospective leader of the free world to get away with the idea that a woman who has an abortion should be punished;
- Support the labeling of an entire ethnic and national group as inferior people;
- Permit the roughhousing of individuals at a political rally as a justifiable act supposedly to

protect "free speech," a diatribe that in itself tears at the fabric of our national unity;

- Accept as a viable candidate for the highest office of our government the very person who callously votes to shut down that government;

- Consider as a viable candidate an individual obsessed with a Messianic complex who feels ordained to save our country;

- Offer for national election either a person who is clearly suffering from a narcissistic personality disorder, or another who fancies himself to be the inflated anointed of God with a special mandate to save the nation by a rule of law not much different from the extremes of the most fanatical religious groups.

How has this happened to us? How have we regressed? What rabbit hole did we fall into that we find ourselves now in a crazy world in which idealism and sacrifice for the common good are ridiculed, while so-called strength of bullying tactics and profit-by-all-means are cheered?

The most common explanations refer to our difficulty recovering from the 2008 recession, our continuing high unemployment, our trade deals, the technological dislocation of people from their workplaces, and the threat of terror attacks hanging over our heads as the "new normal." All of these explanations no doubt impact American consciousness and account for what I am calling a regression, a "dis-ease of our time," but I want to consider a little further that last offering in my list of explanations.

It is not just the threat of terrorism that holds us in a steely grip of fear and prompts a regression of the American mind. Rather, it is the experience of trauma that jarred the American soul and opened the gates for torrents of old barbaric forces to ascend upon our head and heart.

Consider this. The terrorist attacks of 9/11 seared our minds with unforgettable, unthinkable trauma. American Airlines Flight 11 and United Airlines Flight 175 destroyed Manhattan's twin towers, while American Airlines Flight 77 dove into the Pentagon and United Airlines Flight 93 crossed into a rural countryside of Shanksville, Pennsylvania, diverted from its intended target of the White House by a heroic band of passengers who attacked the hijackers of the plane. These events are remembered annually on the now-named Patriot Day when memorial services are held at the sites and names of the victims are read aloud.

The rerun of these scenes on national television, the unforgettable images of people diving to their deaths from the tower, and the devastation of lives, families, and property that followed—all of these linger in our personal and collective memory as scenes from a nightmarish trauma. When we consider that a trauma is "... a disordered psychic or behavioral state resulting from severe mental or emotional stress or physical injury" (*Merriam-Webster*), we may consider how we have all suffered the trauma of 9/11 because we have experienced the disorganized thoughts and emotions that have not been able to make sense of that event. It is beyond our heads and hearts to deal with the utter insanity of the event, and so the insanity of the trauma is internalized. Few of us have been fortunate enough to release the emotions of the 9/11 trauma therapeutically, or to work through the meaning of these meaningless events.

So what happens to our psyches when they respond to the absurdity of such a terror as 9/11? To put it most simply, in the words of W. B. Yeats's poem "The Second Coming," "the center cannot hold." Here is the stanza where we find that line:

> *Turning and turning in the widening gyre*
> *The falcon cannot hear the falconer;*
> *Things fall apart; the centre cannot hold;*
> *Mere anarchy is loosed upon the world,*
> *The blood-dimmed tide is loosed, and everywhere*
> *The ceremony of innocence is drowned;*
> *The best lack all conviction, while the worst*
> *Are full of passionate intensity.*

Although Yeats (1865-1939), as far as I know, did not have in mind the impact of trauma upon the individual psyche, he may well have been musing about the end of an era (Europe before the two world wars) and its traumatic impact upon persons of a spiritual sensibility who witnessed the destructions of their world and culture at the hands of the materialistic/militaristic masses. In any case, I think the image of the center not holding well describes the mind of traumatized persons in their disorganized state as they experience the insane attacks upon a world, its values, and the symbols that are important for a sense of safety and well-being.

And here is the danger that leads to regression. As Yeats puts the matter, when the center does not hold, the best may "lack all conviction," and the worst may emerge with "passionate intensity." In other words, the traumatized mind does not think clearly, and the traumatized heart does not modulate, or regulate, its emotions; the traumatized will of an individual may become vulnerable to the most demonic of leaders.

There are psychic infections just as there are biological ones. There are contagions of mass movements. There are fanaticisms of mass-mindedness. And each of us is susceptible, vulnerable. Jung never ceased to warn us that the eruptions from our deep unconscious in times of great stress have a beguiling power to possess us.

Indeed it is becoming ever more obvious that it
is not famine, not earthquakes, not microbes,
not cancer but man himself who is man's greatest
danger to man, for the simple reason that there is
no adequate protection against psychic epidemics,

which are infinitely more devastating than the worst of natural catastrophes. The supreme danger which threatens individuals as well as whole nations is a psychic danger. Reason has proved itself completely powerless, precisely because its arguments have an effect only on the conscious mind and not on the unconscious. The greatest danger of all comes from the masses, in whom the effects of the unconscious pile up cumulatively and the reasonableness of the conscious mind is stifled. Every mass organization is a latent danger just as much as a heap of dynamite is. It lets loose effects which no man wants and no man can stop. It is therefore in the highest degree desirable that a knowledge of psychology should spread so that man can understand the source of the supreme dangers that threaten them. Not by arming to the teeth, each for itself, can the nations defend themselves in the long run from the frightful catastrophes of modern war. The heaping up of arms is itself a call to war. Rather must they recognize those psychic conditions under which the unconscious bursts the dykes of consciousness and overwhelms it. (CW 18, para. 1358)

A PLACE CALLED HOME

You probably already have images floating across your mind, having read my title above. "Home" means so much. It pulls at our heart, stirs our body, and teases all kinds of thoughts in our heads.

How could "home" not move us so completely? It was one of the first words we learned as children. And it was the place we wanted to come to after we had been away for a spell—a week, a day, an afternoon. "Home" was the place you went for safety, support, understanding, love, and something else—something mysteriously satisfying and meaningful on a level that challenges words to describe it.

By the way, even if your home might have been a painful place, it is altogether likely that in your mind "home" still resonates as a place of refuge and meaning. Maybe even more so!

"Home" is not just a place on a map, not just a place with a zip code, or a place defined by geography. Oh, no!

"Home" is a place in your mind—or better yet—a place in your soul.

For example, take the song "Old Cape Cod" recorded in 1957 by Patty Page. You remember the lyrics?

If you're fond of sand dunes and salty air
Quaint little villages here and there
You're sure to fall in love with old Cape Cod
That old Cape Cod.

If you like the taste of a lobster stew
Served by a window with an ocean view
You're sure to fall in love with old Cape Cod.

Winding roads that seem to beckon you
Miles of green beneath an ocean view
Church bells chimin' on a Sunday morn
Remind you of the town where you were born.

If you spend an evening, you'll want to stay
Watching the moonlight on Cape Cod Bay
You're sure to fall in love with old Cape Cod.
You're sure to fall in love
You're sure to fall in love
With old Cape Cod.

Now the interesting thing about Patty Page's best-selling record of "Old Cape Cod" is this: She had never visited the Cape until after her recording became a big hit. So she visited the place described in those memorable lyrics. And this is how she described her visit to the Cape: "I could not believe it when I finally did go, because I realized that [the song] had captured something about a place that I had had within me for so many years, but never knew. It's unexplainable to me, because it's so dear to me—I knew I had been there before [although] I hadn't" (*Cape Cod Times*, February 27, 2010).

We can understand that, can't we? We find ourselves in some place we have never been, but there is a *déjà vu*! We just seem to know we have been there before. Or it might be that we meet someone, supposedly a stranger, but we feel for sure that we have known that person at some other time!

In other words, something deep within Patty Page resonated with both the words she was singing as well as the actual scenes she experienced when she visited the Cape. There is something in us that is "soulful." Something "deep" calls to "deep." And when we do not allow ourselves to experience it, we become disgruntled, frustrated, manic, or depressed, even sick in body and/or mind, or very susceptible to possibly dangerous distractions.

I have observed this over the years when I visited Cape Cod. The weekends have become almost unbearable with traffic now—people arriving, people leaving. So many people! And why? Of course, we could say they come for a vacation, the food, the beaches, the tourist attractions. There is all of that for the throngs of people filling the highways, streets, shops, and trails.

But there is something more. They lyrics of the song "Old Cape Cod" describe something much deeper than the sentimentality and nostalgia this song can conjure up. Down under that level of feelings, we know we are connecting with the most precious thing of all, what our soul yearns for, what it is to be human—a place called "home."

Remember the movie *E.T.*? E.T., the extraterrestrial, wants to phone home; actually, he wants to return home. It is a brilliant drama of the alien creature who, like each of us, wants to return home. And we found ourselves in the movie wanting so much for E.T. to be able to return to his home. We identify because each of us is E.T. The experience is archetypal, universal, and probably transcends borders of race, culture, species, and extraterrestrial beings.

We feel the stirring of our hearts, the yearnings, and the thought of ways we might attempt to satisfy those yearnings. After all, that is why God gave us summers—so that we might go "home" even if for a little while!

IT'S TIME TO SAY
"HAPPY NEW YEAR"

You may recognize the title of this blog as a line from ABBA's "Happy New Year." But in case you have forgotten or never heard the song, here are the lyrics form the first verse:

> *No more champagne*
> *And the fireworks are through*
> *Here we are, me and you*
> *Feeling lost and feeling blue*
> *It's the end of the party*
> *And the morning seems so gray*
> *So unlike yesterday*
> *Now's the time for us to say ...*

ABBA, the Swedish pop music group that originated in Stockholm in the 1970s, released this hit song in 1980 as part of an album. Against the backdrop of the 1970s, the lyrics above assume an even greater poignancy. With the war in Vietnam, the Iranian Revolution, the conflicts in the Middle East, the rise of terrorism, and the energy/oil crisis, the "party" did seem to be over in many respects.

Apart from the cultural and societal turmoil, ABBA itself would suspend its work, and the two couples in the group would each divorce in the late 70s and early 80s. But this blog is not intended as a psychological analysis of the 70s or of ABBA's psyche, collectively or individually. They appear to have gotten on with life very well.

It is the poignancy of the lyrics in themselves that draws my attention at the moment. Also, there is one additional factor at play for me personally. This comes from a holiday visit with our daughter and her family on the west coast, a visit that gave opportunities for singing and making music with our piano, cello, guitar, tambourines, and voices! This is part of our family tradition. On most occasions when we get together, there will be songs, impromptu performances, laughter, and the challenge of trying new songs to add to our repertoire.

It was at such a moment when we were congratulating ourselves on how well we sounded (to ourselves!) when the suggestion arose that we should do ABBA's "Happy New Year." Sober reflections prevailed, however, and we gently let that prospect for our oeuvre fade away—at least for the moment and perhaps for all time.

Why?

Well, the first and obvious answer is that we could not reach the pinnacle ABBA achieves in their arrangement. But there is something else going on in our reflections on the lyrics of that song. I have referred to the poignancy of the lyrics, but "poignancy" does not contain the deep emotion of the images evoked in those words to the second and third verses:

Sometimes I see
How the brave new world arrives
And I see how it thrives
In the ashes of our lives
Oh yes, man is a fool
And he thinks he'll be okay
Dragging on, feet of clay
Never knowing he's astray
Keeps on going anyway

Seems to me now
That the dreams we had before
Are all dead, nothing now
Than confetti on the floor
It's the end of a decade
in another ten years time
Who can say what we'll find
What lies waiting down the line
In the end of [twenty-nine]

The words are written as if for today. Here we are, you and I, facing a political process in crisis, unending wars of brutalization of armed soldiers and civilians, and an opioid crisis whose real cause has not been named because of what it would reveal about the spiritual vacuousness of our society. We face an upswing in suicide rates for our children and young people, the creeping ecological changes, the destruction of habitats for wildlife and humans who migrate to our neighborhoods and shores, and the engines that drive our production and marketing of distractions that anesthetize our consciences.

But ABBA's song does not end in despair, and neither must we resign ourselves to the distressing way of things we are experiencing as an old year ends and a new year begins. We are free to envision another world, a kinder and more hopeful world. Here is the way ABBA ends their lyrics:

> *Happy new year*
> *Happy new year*
> *May we all have a vision now and then*
> *Of a world where every neighbor is a friend*
> *Happy new year*
> *Happy new year*
> *May we all have our hopes, our will to try*
> *If we don't we may as well lay down and die*
> *You and I*

I am choosing to believe the party is not over, that all of our dreams are not like confetti on the floor, and that we do not have to stand on feet of clay, because our feet are made for dancing!

I invite you to join me in the dance, as I wish you a happy new year!

CHAPTER FOUR

ULTIMATE MEANING

*In the midst of winter, I found there was, within me,
an invincible summer. And that makes me happy.
For it says that no matter how hard the world
pushes against me, within me, there's something
stronger—something better, pushing right back.*
—A. Camus

MEDITATION AND
A GREAT PARADOX

In my consultation room where I conduct my clinical practice, hardly a day goes by that I do not come up against a great paradox. It is this: *The more we change, the more we remain the same.* I am borrowing here from a French proverb stated first by the novelist Alphonse Karr (1808–1890) but adapting it for use in a very personal and clinical way.

Let me give you some examples of what I mean. A well-educated and professional woman in her 50s fears the rapidly changing business environment of her profession in which she has been very successful. She tells me she feels she "does not belong" either in her professional group or her greater community. It is a thought she has been aware of since early childhood when her parents moved up their professional ladders rapidly, which meant she was always "the new kid" in the schools and communities where her family would move. The more she changed, growing older, moving around, the more she remained the same.

Then there is the executive in his 40s who is very bright but fears each day of his work life, particularly following promotions to new levels of his work, that he will be found out and exposed for who he really is. When I ask him what that is, he tells me that he is "stupid." The more he is promoted, the more "stupid" he feels because his duties are more complex, and he thinks he should understand everything about them because everyone else does, and the reason he does not is because he's "stupid." "And when did you conclude you are stupid?" I asked.

Of course, his answer would not surprise any adult who has suffered through the trauma of those early classes in math, reading, science, etc., especially given the merciless pressure of our peer groups and the cruel inadequacy of some teachers. The executive with whom I was working also struggled with a particular learning disorder that made math especially hard for him, and in those school classes, he concluded that he was stupid. He said the other kids in his class would quickly grasp the concepts in math, and his classmates would laugh at him when he was asked to work a problem on the chalkboard.

One more example. This is a lady in her 50s who tells me she has been married three times and is considering leaving her present husband. The reason, she goes on to tell me, is because he withdraws from her to the point where they have no intimacy. When I inquire more deeply, I find out that something like this also happens with her friends. She has no close friends; they either leave or let me down, she says.

Then she becomes angry with them and eventually goes on to find a new friend whom she idealizes until that one also lets her down and she becomes angry again. In this way, she cycles through her husbands and friends. The more she tries, she says, the more she is betrayed, just like she was hurt by her mother and father who could never be counted on to consistently "be there" for her when she wanted to be held and loved as a child.

In her ever-changing world, this lady remains more and more the same: hurt, "betrayed" (in her mind), abandoned and abandoning, hopeful and then disillusioned. As in the first example, the more the woman's professional world changed, the more she felt she did not belong. And with the male executive, the more he was promoted, the more stupid he thought himself to be.

This is a great paradox, as I am describing it. It is the phenomenon that the more we change, the more we remain the same.

But notice with me what is actually going on here. Yes, the world is changing; yes, each of us is aging and thus experiencing all those changes that occur in our bodies as the years go by. And, yes, the Buddhists approach this reality of fundamental change in their doctrine of impermanence (*anicca*) that is summarized poetically in George Harrison's song "All Things Must Pass, All Things Must Pass Away."

However, that is not quite true when it comes to our inner lives, is it? As my wife reminds her young cello students,

"Practice does not necessarily make perfect; practice makes permanent." In other words, while change takes place all around us and within us, the psychological truth is that the mind carries within itself some very basic core beliefs that may be permanent for our lifetime. These are the thoughts such as those I described in the three examples above. These thoughts—"I do not belong," "I am stupid," and "Everyone I try to get close to disappoints me"—are "practiced" several times a day. Within the old neural pathways of our brain, they have become permanent. We created them in our earliest thoughts, and now they form the psychological reality within which we live.

Until we don't. And this brings me to meditation. Have you ever closely reflected on those marvelous Zen photographs or drawings of landscapes? I am talking here, for example, about the scenes that portray a calm mountain lake, perhaps surrounded by trees, with a clear moon likely reflected on the still water. I wondered many times in the past when I looked at these peaceful scenes, why are there no human beings or animals in them? And the reason is this. The photographer or artist is not simply trying to create a work of aesthetic beauty. Rather, the pictures are attempts to reveal the mind in repose, the natural mind before it is taken over by repetitive thoughts that actually are a maladaptive interpretation of inner images or environmental events.

This is a snapshot of the "Zen mind." Those old, disturbing thoughts are not running on automatic. The world has stopped. The "change" of the world is held within a moment of eternity, and the "permanent" thought of an old conclusion has dissolved. To experience this sense of timelessness and clarity is to descend to the very ground of our being.

Try it. Sit comfortably in your chair. Close your eyes. Take three or four deep breaths and then resume normal breathing while you let your body progressively relax. Sink into your chair. Suspend your worries for the moment. Clear your mind by bringing your attention to your relaxed breathing. Notice the pleasant sensations arising in your body. Observe the peacefulness that comes when, even for one second, you let your mind realize its natural state of clarity before your "monkey mind" starts the tape player all over again—as it will!

Do not be anxious or impatient. The more you do this, the more you become mindful of a great paradox: the essential self we are as we grow and change. This is the promise of mindful meditation.

THE LOST SYMBOL:
A SIGN OF OUR TIMES

My cat Sheba understands signals very well. When either my wife or I sit on the floor in the evening before going to bed, it means "play time!" Chase the string, jump at the tethered "fly" overhead, bat the rolling ball, and so forth. She may modify the routine as we go along, much like Calvin and Hobbes from their comic strip days, but it's all in the realm of play.

Cats, dogs, and other animals quickly learn the signals for play, food, sleep, a walk, and—unfortunately—for that infamous trip to the vet, or the family vacation, which means they go to the kennel, at which time our Sheba becomes the great Ninja! She disappears, fades into her latest hiding place, and resists all efforts to capture her when she eventually is found.

We can see their intelligence and emotions in response to the signals we send. And, of course, this signaling works both ways, doesn't it? Sheba "signals" to us when she is hungry, tired, sleepy, angry, sick, stalking, playful, or wanting to cuddle.

But, as far as we know, animals do not understand symbols. I am moving here toward a distinction between symbols, signs, and signals. It is true that in our culture, presently, these words most often are used interchangeably and with little attention to the deeper nuances of "symbol." So it is interesting, if I am following this development clearly, that a major concern in the field of Artificial Intelligence has to do with this issue of transforming a signal into a symbol. The underlying thought regarding robotic intelligence regards the working of the mind as a mechanical, computational process in which electrical impulses could be transformed into a kind of rational reckoning.

But this usage of "symbol" would more accurately describe a "sign." This is an important distinction particularly in the fields of religion, philosophy, and psychoanalysis. A sign is an "indicator" of something known. The "indicator" holds no mystery, no uncertainty, no question. The movement of thought from indicator to subject is generally a linear one of direct correspondence. In the case of a traffic light, the color green in our culture means "go," red means "stop," and yellow means "caution." We read the sign and respond. No questions.

Obviously, then, signs are important. We need them to function in the service of regulating traffic flow in our society, whether it be vehicular traffic, or the flow of communication between and among groups of people, or between machines and humans. But signs are not symbols.

Symbols are "… the best possible expression for something unknown—bridges thrown out toward an unseen shore" (*CW 15,* para. 116). As such, the symbol serves to make a connection between the conscious and the unconscious. In other words, the symbol defies easy explanation because it is rooted within the human unconscious that has a grip on us mentally and emotionally. Quite likely, the symbolic image grasps our attention and, in some cases, possesses us. Think of the scenes we see daily in our media where individuals and groups move within a frenzied state of mind to commit bizarre acts of violence on others. Or, again, consider the frenetic titillation of money and prizes of TV game shows, the "to-die-for" creations of ad agencies, the euphoric mascots at college and professional sports events, and the fascination with vampires, aliens, extraterrestrials, and conspiracies. How can we be so gullible?

And the answer is found back in the nature of symbols. They arise out of the unconscious and evoke a deep emotional resonance. They coalesce around emotion, thought, and body sensation; they make possible the experience of some kind of meaning in that the symbols arise from the central theme in the unconscious having to do with the centuries-long adventures of risk-taking, life, death, love, and loss. But let us remember also that symbols may lose their potency over the course of time.

At that point when a symbol "dies" (loses its potency and meaningfulness), a dry formalism, sterility, or dogma develops. Adherents may still feel loyalty to the old symbols and feel duty-bound to pay allegiance, becoming more radical and extreme as the formerly live symbol fades over the horizon into the past. This is not just in the case of religion but in all "–isms" that control the minds of people.

In the examples I have given, my emphasis was on the efficacy or potency that symbols possess, even when they appeal to our darker side. I don't mean to suggest that symbols are to be associated only with what appears sometimes as an incessant need for stimulation. In fact, the symbols may also arise out of reverence, awe, and the highest ideals of our people. We see some of these in the great religions and in profound political acts of courage and justice. Even in these cases, the symbols may fade and die. Individuals, groups, and even societies may become fallow and vacuous, a condition of dryness that feels like death.

But then a very liberating phenomenon may occur. It may be the appearance of a dream that challenges the old order and seizes individuals or groups with an image that stirs new life. The dream may be a very personal one or one of epic proportion. Consider the conversion of Emperor Constantine to Christianity in 312 C.E. How did this come to be? The details of this pivotal development in European history are sketchy and pieced together from the records of a

Roman historian, Eusebius, and an advisor to Constantine, Lactantius.

The general narrative that has come down to us is known as "The Battle of the Milvian Bridge" and goes like this. On the evening of October 27, 312, Constantine faced the most significant battle of his life, one that would determine the next emperor of the Roman Empire. Constantine's rival, Maxentius, occupied Rome; the developing battle likely would be fought at the Milvian Bridge, which straddled the Tiber River and controlled access to Rome. On that evening of the 27th, Constantine saw a vision in the sky that was confirmed by a dream in which "he saw the initial letters of the name of Christ with the words, 'By this sign you will conquer'" (Eusebius). Constantine painted the monogram *Chi Rho* on his helmet as well as on his shield and those of his soldiers (Walker, p. 101).

Constantine won the battle; Maxentius was defeated, and Constantine became not only the ruler of the Roman Empire but a Christian convert who rescinded the edits that had depersonalized Christians. In a move that changed the direction of world history, Constantine's new "Edict of Milan" granted absolute freedom to all citizens in the empire, opening the door for future developments in which the Christian Church would eventually share power with the state.

Such a dramatic appearance of a symbol is not an everyday occurrence. But, on the other hand, we do not know. We are so conditioned to disregard our dreams, and the professions of psychiatry, psychotherapy, clinical psychology, and psychoanalysis have become so preoccupied with neuroscience and the atomization of clinical studies in general that little attention is given to the narratives and images of the waking and sleeping mind. Meanwhile, on the other side of the street, organized religion has become obsessed with defending its doctrines, growing in numbers with megachurches while aligning with right-wing power politics.

The spirit of the times is preoccupied with the signs of the times. This is part of the barbarism of our age that will end only when the pendulum swings back and we learn yet again the difference between a signal, a sign, and a symbol.

THE DELIBERATE LIFE: MORE ON DREAMS AND MEDITATION

The story is told about the fox who chases a rabbit. As the story goes, the rabbit eludes the fox who might have been faster. So how did this happen? The fox was pursuing its dinner but the terrified rabbit was running for its life.
(*Hyams, p. 123*)

Let's think about the fox and the rabbit in this story as parts of ourselves. Let's also consider these animals in the narrative as symbols for the way we focus our attention. The fox focuses attention on satisfying his/her appetite; the rabbit turns attention to his/her life. For the purposes of the point I am making here, I think it would be accurate to say that the rabbit moves with some greater degree of urgency. This is "deliberation" as the dictionary defines it: "done with or marked by full consciousness of the nature and effects" (*American Heritage Dictionary*). As we shall see, the way we focus our attention determines the way we live our lives—with deliberation or not.

These are the choices I am attempting to put forth when I talk and write about dreams and meditation. For I am not promoting dreams and meditation as ways to become better foxes—more efficient, more powerful, more able to gain one-upmanship over others. Nor am I hyping dreams and meditation as paths of devotion to become better persons. Actually, any of the above may result from intentional work with dreams and meditation.

I would hope that our lives would increase with efficiency and productivity in the world, as well as with a deepening of one's spiritual being.

However, I am approaching the practices of dreams and meditation with the intent of transcending the dualisms of life that split us internally and separate us from one another. I maintain an understanding and practice of dreams and meditation in line with the schools of martial arts that have influenced those teachers committed to the unity of body-mind-spirit, with rootedness in the daily affairs of life where there are conflicts, fragmentation, violence, and oppositions within and without.

This is not just meditation and dreams as an activity attached to our already too-busy lives. Rather, it is the work with dreams and meditation that become a way of life lived with deliberation. It is a way of life marked by moral intention, the exercise of power with others rather than over or under them, a recognition of love as the great force that straddles life and death, and the recognition of meaning as the grand outcome of living which—it may be—only we human beings bring to the network of stars making up our universe. It is a way of life described by Lao-Tzu:

> *A man is born gentle and weak.*
> *At his death he is hard and stiff.*
> *Green plants are tender and filled with sap.*
> *At their death they are withered and dry.*
> *Therefore the stiff and unbending is the disciple*
> *of death.*
> *The gentle and yielding is the disciple of life.*
> *Thus an army without flexibility never wins a*
> *battle.*
> *A tree that is unbending is easily broken.*
> *The hard and the strong will fall.*
> *The soft and the weak will overcome.*

I think Lao-Tzu is using the metaphor of "hard" and "stiff" to suggest an attitude that is rigid, critical, and closed. On the other hand, there is the gentle and yielding attitude that takes into account the fullness of life, the diversity, even the many voices that occupy the mind of each of us—an attitude open and expectant that greets each day with the surprises of potentialities, creativity, and connectedness with all creatures. At the core, we are one with ourselves; at the core, we are one with others and all being. At the core, we realize that life not lived with deliberation is a waste. Running from the fox, the rabbit reaches down into a deeper core where life is precious and moves with deliberate speed.

But, obviously, to get to that core, we have to deal with the many voices that buffer us within; we have to acknowledge the many faces we present to the world at different times. How can we know these things? How can we become aware of this diversity within? This is the focus of our dreamwork that reveals all that we are.

And how can we still these many voices within us? How can we cope with the tempest that rages within and without? This is the task of our meditation.

Through our dreams and in our meditations, we come to ourselves. And only then are we able to take our rightful place in our very troubled world, with wisdom, power, peace, and happiness.

> *For the uncontrolled, there is no wisdom,*
> *nor for the uncontrolled is there the power of*
> *concentration; and for him without concentration*
> *there is no peace. And for the unpeaceful, how*
> *can there be happiness?*
> *(Bhagavad Gita, Discourse 2, verse 66)*

DREAMS AND MEDITATION: THE FIELD OF CONFLICT

H ere is a dream for us to reflect upon:

> *I am with a friend in some place, very familiar to*
> *me, but one I can't identify. We have been given a*
> *mission, but nothing is clear, neither what we are to*
> *do, nor where we are to go. I walk out in the street*
> *but feel very scared. My friend is no longer with me.*

The dreamer is a very intelligent professional woman in her early 60s, with some notable accomplishments behind her. Yet, sometimes, she feels seized by fear, afraid she will be overcome by her anxiety and fall into shame and ridicule because of some mistake she might make. Her religion has brought great comfort in the past, enabling her to carry on. But because she is bright and curious, she wants to understand her dilemma and has moved into practices of meditation and dreamwork. This led to our discussion of how, from my psychoanalytic practice and insight, we might approach her work with dreams and meditation with even more depth, understanding, and focus of practice.

So let's think about what her dream may be communicating and what implications—if any—the dream may have for her and us as well. When I asked her about the context of the dream, what had occurred around the time of the dream, nothing stood out. This suggested that the dream, as is often the case, did not refer back to a specific experience in waking life but was formed in childhood and which might be continuing in her present life, taking the form of a mood, a feeling tone, or what we might call a psychological complex.

I asked how that kind of drama appeared in her childhood. In other words, did you have times when you felt confused about what was expected of you, or how to do things in an approving way, or how to make sense of what the parents said and did? This is an important part of a child's life: to **understand** what is going on, what one is expected to do, how to do it, how to deal with so many things like acts of violence that make no sense to a child. Second, to be given **support** with tasks and with coping when feeling overwhelmed. Third, to be **nurtured** through the challenging stages of development and performances of schoolwork and tests, as well as the onslaught of social expectation. Lastly, to be **guided** not only by words but by actions toward adult ways of modulating scary experiences.

Of those four major ways to care for children in their interactions with conflictual situations in life, the dreamer could recall very few instances during her childhood when she received such care. It was not that her parents were sinister and mean. In fact, they would have insisted that they loved their daughter and told her that her family was "a loving family." But that was not so. The mother and father wanted to be loving and tried to show "love" by buying things, taking trips, and maintaining an obedient relationship with their parents who, it turns out, were abusive in their methods of discipline and general absence of showing affection, respect, and safety.

So, it was a family drama. In the dream, we could see the parts of the drama as they circled through the generations: fear, not feeling safe, not fully understanding what was going on and what to do, not witnessing healthy modulation of conflict and fear, feeling alone with no one to talk to and no one to be counted on for protection.

Thus, although nothing specific came to the dreamer's mind as a situation that may have prompted the dream, upon closer questioning the dreamer did bring to mind a situation at work in which she did not feel safe psychologically, a situation in which she may have felt ashamed by her level of "performance" and all alone in dealing with her feelings. But note that this situation was not noted as significant! Why, because it is the way of feeling and experiencing life that has become habitual for the dreamer. It is the "soup" she swims in regularly and expects nothing else!

How does this occur? And how is this pattern changed? These are the fundamental questions in psychotherapy. But not only are these the questions, they are the first stage of a recovery and further realization of the fullness of one's life—one's Original Self brought into consciousness through the process Carl Jung called individuation. This means that whatever may have thrown us off our path of personhood that is unique, productive, and meaningful, it is still possible to overcome those dysfunctional functions and develop healthy ways of being in the world in line with our particular potentialities. This is our human potential realized.

Why can I say that? Because of the feature of the brain that is referred to as its "plasticity." Old patterns of functioning depend upon the circuit established between the amygdala and cortex of our brain. The signals picked up in the environment set in motion the process in the circuit of cortex/amygdala interaction that allows for feelings of danger to prompt cognitions and actions that result in a replay of the originating drama. In the case of the dreamer, she is in a situation that demands some level of performance, of which she is insecure; from there she feels "exposed" (on the street) and alone with no one to help her. That drama is encoded within her brain, and any threatening situation with similar circumstance that could be perceived as the same basic condition will activate the old pattern.

That is our bio-neurological heritage, and it was a good one. It helped us survive over many centuries when we had to cope with wild beasts, a shortage of food, a small band of supporters, and a threatening environment. The brain enabled us to identify danger, remember the situation, and take quick action to survive. I jump when I see a limb lying on the ground in my backyard at night, thinking it is a snake, and only after taking the action of jumping back in fear do I realize it is only a limb.

The brain assists us, but now we must assist the brain. Note how it does two things that are especially significant. First, on the bio-neurological level, it encodes situations of urgency for survival and well-being. Second, extending the bio-neurological to the psychological level of processing, images are sent to us via our dreams. As with the person whose dream we have been considering, each of us receives such messages nightly. And as with her, we can glean very valuable information from our dreams: We can identify those "states of mind" that describe distressing, dysfunctional ways of thinking, feeling, and acting. In her case, we have identified a sequence of dynamics as they occurred in childhood, repeated in her daily life, and now told in the story of her dream.

What do we do with these dreams? This is the point where dreams and meditation come together. This is, one may say, a meditation that might be described as preparation for entering the "field of conflict." In this case, we are intentionally bringing the mind to focus on entering the very kind of situation that has brought fear to the dreamer.

These are the steps:

1.   Begin by practicing meditation as learning to
     relax and training the attention to hold the one
     point. This is crucial because in the childhood
     experiences where one's attention was fragmented
     by being overwhelmed by fear, there was no way
     the child could hold her attention, concentrate,
     and modulate her feelings. So the basic
     meditation of relaxing and training the attention
     is the beginning point.

2.   Next, the meditation uses desensitization to
     enter the field of conflict. Holding the attention
     with the steadiness of a sword's one point, insert
     yourself into the situation that causes fear.
     Coordinate the deep breathing, remain relaxed,
     and envision yourself entering the field of conflict
     with calm, power, and focused attention. If the
     situation becomes too frightening, leave the scene,
     recompose yourself, and re-enter again. Do not
     worry if this takes days, weeks, months. You have
     spent a lifetime living in the shadow of the fear, so
     do not expect that you will quickly overcome that
     old fear. Pace yourself and feel your determined
     resolve.

3. Call upon your allies. Call to mind religious
    figures who inspire you and give you strength
    such as Jesus, the Buddha, St. Paul, Krishna, or
    some present-day individual who brings calm and
    a sense of reassuring power to your mind when
    you think of them. Remember, the psyche makes
    possible the presence of persons and powers that
    accompany you and are available for counsel and
    support. Let them enter the scene with you when
    you meditate on entering the field of conflict.

It is here at this point within us where dreams and meditation intersect that we find who we really are and what really
matters to us. From this point, our lives take on renewed
meaning.

*Once upon a time, several knights rode their horses
into the dark woods, in search of a very valuable
message with healing information for the world
that had been stolen and was reported to be located
in a castle far beyond the woods. A young aspiring
knight observed each of the knights departing, but
each entering at a different point in the woods.
Feeling anxious for the knights, the young man in
training turned to his teacher who had trained the
knights. "How can they possibly find the castle?"
he asked. "The woods are very deep and dark; they*

may die in the woods because they do not know where the castle is. Aren't you scared for them?" The master replied, *"No, I am not scared for them."* *"Why not?"* the young man asked. The master *looked compassionately at the trail of the knights now hidden by the woods and said, "They do not know where the castle is, but they know where they are."* (Source Unknown)

AN END TO SUFFERING? (PART 1)

We have just had to euthanize our petite, black and white tuxedo cat. A faithful, dutiful companion for going-on 19 years, Sheba was strong, loyal, and courageous to the end. We had battled a melanoma on her lower-left lip for three years. The melanoma won, but not until after we had thrown everything at it that we possibly could: immunotherapy, radiation, chemotherapy, and herbal medicines and painkillers. We kept her alive so long because she seemed herself to be choosing life: eating, bathing, and going for walks in our yard until the last three days when she finally refused medicines and food. So, we held her and tearfully uttered our goodbyes while she was mercifully attended by a most compassionate vet who specializes in hospice and euthanasia in the home.

Sheba's suffering and death parallel some pages in a manuscript I am attempting to complete. The focus on this manuscript does not arise out of the blue. The theme of suffering nestles within my twin vocations of Pastoral Counseling and Jungian Analysis. How could the experience of suffering not occupy some central place within the work of all practitioners of healing? Suffering is life; life is suffering, although not the only thing.

But just because suffering holds center stage in each developmental phase of life, precisely because of its prominence in human existence, we desperately attempt to not see the ravages of suffering. We try to drag it behind the curtain of life's drama. We distract ourselves with diversions of anything we can buy, beg, borrow, or burglarize—anything that will take our minds off the real truth of our finite existence.

That truth is this: All that rises falls away. Siddhartha Gautama (563–483 B.C.E), a young nobleman living in a border area between what is now India and Nepal, woke up to the reality of life's suffering in his observations of birth, aging, disease, death, and the experience of the loss of loved ones and things. This realization of life's impermanence and suffering was too much for Gautama. If this is all life is about, he appears to have reasoned, then how can we live with such awareness? Maybe more importantly, why continue on with life if we cannot escape or end the suffering?

And so, on the night of his 29th birthday, Gautama abandoned his life of luxury and privilege to become a wandering ascetic in search of an end to suffering. After six years, following an in-depth encounter with Mara, the tempter who traffics in distractions, diversions, and delusions of life, Gautama realized the enlightenment of his "Buddha-nature."

Emerging from his six years of an ascetic quest, a life-and-death encounter with Mara, the demon of unconsciousness, and finally a heroic affirmation of an enlightened conquest of suffering, the Buddha preached his first sermon at Deer Park in Sarnath, India. It was here Siddhartha Gautama, now speaking as the Buddha, announced an end to suffering, or at least, the way by which an individual might experience an end to suffering. As the very foundation of what would become Buddhism, the fourth largest of the major religions today, Buddha taught his small group of listeners the "Four Noble Truths" and the "Noble Eightfold Path." These, he said, reveal the path to end suffering for all who honor these truths. In a brief summary, they may be described like this:

FOUR NOBLE TRUTHS

1. *The truth of suffering.* Human existence is marked by the nature of impermanence, which we experience in birth, aging, disease, death, and the loss of all things and persons we hold dear.

2. *The truth of the cause of suffering.* The cause comes from the manifold feelings, thoughts, and sensations of anxiety that arise from our recognition of and attempt to avoid suffering, our drives to attach to things and persons we want to possess, and our pursuit of the countless

distractions that divert our attention from suffering.

3. *The truth of the cessation of suffering.* It is not inevitable that we suffer, says the Buddha. In fact, there is a cessation to this suffering.

4. *The truth of the Noble Eightfold Path.* The cessation of suffering may be experienced through the intentionality of following the Eightfold Path as described below.

NOBLE EIGHTFOLD PATH

1. *Right understanding.* The word "right" as used here is not to be understood moralistically. "Right" refers to that which is appropriate to the situation. Thus, "right" understanding means that the Noble Eightfold Path begins with a conscious acknowledgement of the reality of suffering interwoven within the essence of existence.

2. *Right intention.* The right intention is to undertake the Noble Eightfold Path of one's own choosing with a resolve to see it through, recognizing the Path will likely lead us into new discoveries of our old "self" while opening up unexplored, new ways of being in the world.

3. *Right speech.* Our words arise from our thoughts; indeed, they are our thoughts. "As persons think in their hearts, so they will be." What comes out is what is within, yes? But the reverse is also true: What we say takes lodging within us. Our speech arises from our character while at the same time our words continue to mold our character. How hard it is in some families to say to one another, "I love you." However, once spoken, the ice begins to melt, and a new relationship is born.

4. *Right action.* The same that was said about our speech applies as well to our actions. When people come into my consulting room, wanting to deal with a conflict in personal relationships or difficulties in the workplace, they will sometimes say, "But this is just the way I am!" To which I gently remind them, "No, this is the way you have learned to be." If you change your behavior, you create a new life, and from your new life, you change the world.

5. *Right vocation.* I am not talking about your job as such; I am referring to your "calling" to be in the world—which may be expressed in many different "jobs."

6. *Right effort.* The Buddha spoke of "effort" in four steps: (a) awareness of the negative pattern

of thinking; (b) a resolve to turn loose that old pattern; (c) awareness of a new way of thinking; (d) commitment to put that new way of thinking into practice. This "new way" is that which leads to health and the alleviation of suffering.

7. *Right mindfulness.* We are likely to associate this with meditation, "mindfulness meditation." In that meditation, we watch our thoughts, feelings, and sensations arise, pass by, and then go on over the horizon of our consciousness. But right mindfulness does not end with our meditation, nor is it intended to. We learn in our meditation to practice in our active life the process of being mindful of feelings, thoughts, sensations. Our anger, our fear, and our moods arise as we encounter stressful situations and people. But we learn we have choices: We do not have to attach to any of those feelings, thoughts, or sensations. We may need to take action, even strong action in some cases, but we do our best in mindfulness training to learn how to respond consciously. We have the feelings or thoughts; they do not have us.

8. *Right concentration.* This one is hard because it refers to that which is wordless. Consider its etymology, *centrum* from Latin, meaning "center." And look at the definitions Webster gives us:

1. to bring or direct toward a common center;

2. to render less diffuse, less dilute;

3. to express the essence of;

4. to bring all one's powers, faculties, or activities to bear;

5. to direct the attentions of the mental faculties toward a single object [the "one point"].

This brings us to a deeper state of meditation. It is in the state of concentration that bliss may arise. It is in this culmination of the Noble Eightfold Path that Buddha would say we realize our true humanity as a connection to the universe and to all others who, like us, suffer, but now with a sense of meaningfulness—perhaps. This is the "end" of all the major religions, as it is the "end" of suffering.

AN END TO SUFFERING?
(PART 2)

In my previous blog on suffering, I described the suffering of our precious, 19-year-old cat, Sheba, who died of a melanoma that viciously attacked her mouth. I also described the excruciating suffering my wife and I endured as we treated Sheba's cancer and as we held her at the end when our vet euthanized her at home. Even as I write this, some four weeks later, I cannot hold back the tears—thinking of her death, how noble and present she was to us until her last breath.

So there we were, intimately facing what is inevitable for each of us, death. And suffering—the suffering of birth, aging, disease, the loss of all things and persons we hold dear, and then death. In my last blog, I described how Siddhartha Gautama, who became the Buddha, found unbearable this cycle of birth and death, and how he discovered an "end" to suffering through a realization of the Four Noble Truths and the Noble Eightfold Path. This is Buddhism's understanding of the human potential to experience "an end to suffering."

And what do the Christians propose? Or, more particularly, what did Jesus say? I was mulling over that question soon after Sheba's death when a friend told me about his loss of a pet. My friend told me how he greatly empathized with us because he had been through that experience himself and could not believe the depth of the pain. In fact, he said, "I believe I have grieved more deeply over my pet's death than the death of my mother and father!" A number of people have told me something of the same thing—how they find it hard to admit that the grief over losing a precious pet aches so deeply. As my friend and I pondered that experience, he paused and said very thoughtfully, "Actually, that love my cat showed me might have been the closest I have ever come to experiencing unconditional love."

His statement surprised me. My friend is not a person who appears to be in touch with his feelings in general. He does not appear to be curious about his inner world, or if so, he is either reticent to talk about it or does not have the words to express what he may think and feel deeply. But there it came out—with his cat he experienced unconditional love, a bond between them that seemed not to be limited by conditions.

"Unconditional love," I pondered. That probably does capture the bond my wife and I shared with Sheba. Even when I could sometimes feel irritated with her and speak more sharply than usual, she would return in a forgiving manner to curl up comforting me. Sure, I thought, this is all about her thinking about her next meal; this is all about eating and sleeping and doing it all again the next day! But I knew better.

Yes, we can anthropomorphize; we can project our human cognitions, motives, and emotions upon our pets. But to reduce our understanding of the bond between human beings and pets as a relationship of co-dependent survival behaviors is to rob the attachment bond of a transcendent meaning that enriches our existence. And now we can take a step even further, thanks to the increasing research in animals' behavior and brains.

Now we can define and describe empathy in many species; now we can trace the human compassionate instinct through an evolutionary process that moves "from the bottom up," informing our consciousness of an instinct we may call compassion or empathy that is not only within a species but also between species.

This "attachment bond" may carry many names. Among human beings we call it *love*. And within the Christian community, the name of that love is *agape*. It is almost common knowledge today to refer to our Greek heritage that has helped us distinguish between the different forms of love, including: *philautia* (self-love), *pragma* (a practical bond of attachment that may describe some long marriages), *storge* (tenderness and affection such as parents feel toward children), *philia* (a bond between friends), *eros* (a drive toward union with that which is desired), and *agape* (unconditional love that "wills the good of another," as described by Thomas Aquinas).

Furthermore, C. S. Lewis offered us the keen insight in his book *The Four Loves* that "the highest good does not stand without the lowest." I take this to mean that *agape* does not assume some sanctimonious perch separate from the other forms of love but rather enfolds them in an embrace of a wholistic consciousness. This is what compels *agape* toward an unconditional regard for all sentient beings.

And this is the compelling theme in the New Testament. God is defined as *agape* (1 John 4:8 and 4:16). Also, drawing upon his Hebraic heritage as described in Deuteronomy 6 and Leviticus 19, Jesus describes the Great Commandment in this way: "Love (*agape*) the Lord your God with all your heart and with all your soul and with all your mind. And the second is like it: Love (*agape*) your neighbor as yourself" (Matthew 22:36–39, RSV). Then, just before his death, Jesus gave his disciples what he called "a new commandment": "that you love (*agape*) one another. Just as I have loved (*agape*) you, you also are to love (*agape*) one another" (John 13:34, EST).

This is the essence of Christianity. Its gift to the world is a witness to the meaning of love that is unconditional, whose name is *agape*, whose motivating force nudges humanity on toward what Teilhard de Chardin calls the Omega Point (*CW 9ii*, para. 190ff), an evolutionary destiny of life in which the conscious and unconscious meet to provide humankind with a deep morality that guides us beyond the Freudian super-ego toward the laws of life itself and the God within.

Of course, Christianity's demonstration of *agape* down through the centuries has been compromised by humanity's failure to protect the little ones, by a wretched abuse of power that has destroyed habitats, by a tendency to side with dictators who use power to dominate others, by a prejudice against women who are equated with the source of so-called "original sin" based upon a misinterpretation of Eve's role in the creation myth, and by an anthropomorphic hubris that demeans other creatures in our beloved animal kingdom. Yes, all of that is true, and all of that—and more—debases the principle of *agape*. It is enough to drive each of us who have been baptized within that tradition to hang our heads in shame.

How ironical it is then that we see in the eyes of our pets a forgiving unconditional love. True, it may not be what we fully mean by *agape*. Our pets, our dogs, cats, birds, and other creatures do not have the same brain structure we have. And we must not be naïve in overlooking their instincts for survival, instincts of territoriality and mating, hunger and hunting, aggression and fear of aggression. These are our instincts as well, although played out in what we may rationalize as a more civilized manner. Still, the force of unconditional love in these creatures drives us toward an introspection by which we are made more deeply human.

Here at this point in my writing, two synchronicities occurred which I would like to share with you. The first synchronicity is the irritating peck on the wooden structure of my house by the downy woodpecker looking for a suitable home. Typically, the downy woodpecker establishes a nest in trees of which we have plenty around our house, so many we have not provided a substitute nest—yet.

And so, when the woodpecker comes along, checking out my house, I find I also have to contend with another uninvited guest—my most Elmer Fudd-like self who marches outside to do battle with the petite downy woodpecker. The bird seems to find this charade of competition over a choice of homes to be amusing. I rush outside; it flies up in a tree and patiently waits for me to go back inside so that we can repeat this maneuver several times, amidst threats and pecks and slamming doors and flapping wings. We are planning to buy a house—for the woodpecker—this next week.

Now, the second synchronicity. Taking a break from my writing, over breakfast this morning and my weekly read of *The New York Times' Book Review* (February 26, 2019), I was surprised to see on the front page a review of Dr. Frans de Waal's latest book, *Mama's Last Hug*.

De Waal is a Dutch-born primatologist whose research and writing have opened doors in my mind to the reality of emotions in animals. The reviewer, Sy Montgomery, describes one passage in de Waal's book when two old friends met after some time had passed:

The two old friends hadn't seen each other lately.
Now one of them was on her deathbed, crippled
with arthritis, refusing food and drink, dying of
old age. Her friend had come to say goodbye.
At first she didn't seem to notice him. But when
she realized he was there, her reaction was
unmistakable: Her face broke into an ecstatic grin.
She cried out in delight. She reached for her visitor's
hand and stroked his hair. As he caressed her face,
she draped her arm around his neck and pulled
him closer.

In this moving real-life scene, the "friend" who is visiting is the Dutch biologist, Dr. Jan van Hooff, and he is visiting his old friend, Mama, a chimpanzee.

I think the last moments with Sheba were much the same. And these shared moments are happening now all around the globe. It may not be *agape,* but it is a bond of love that crosses the bridge of our separateness, a bond in which our suffering, regardless of our religion or politics, is eclipsed by a greater reality.

GLOSSARY

Sources consulted are listed below.

AHD — *American Heritage Dictionary*
EHB — *Encyclopedia of Human Behavior*
OAD — *Oxford American Dictionaries*
RM — My personal synthesis: Randall Mishoe
WHO — World Health Organization

archetype: primal forms of being arising from evolutionary origins, manifesting in human beings as universal patterns of behavior, cognition, emotion, and perception; or as images that appear in dreams, symbols, and myths; or as deeply felt experiences and encounters that are meaningful but not necessarily explicable through present-day paradigms; functioning in the human unconscious as formative centers of psychological complexes; capable of constellating a psychoid field of connectivity. **(RM)**

character: a person's identity, self-perceived and/ or recognized by others, distinguished by beliefs, behavioral patterns, typology, temperament, morals, patterns of relationship, and general attitude toward oneself and the outer world. **(RM)**

complex: often referred to as "sub-personalities," "splinter psyches," or "a mood," and manifesting as a felt experience of psychic energy that brings with it a particular feeling tone, thought/cognitions, perceptions accompanied by possible changes in body sensations and processes, a shift in self-perception that may be quite subtle or appear even as another personality, and lasting for a few seconds or an extended period of time. **(RM)**

conscious: used in Jungian psychology as an adjective to connote awareness, and as a noun to describe that part of the psyche that is not unconscious. **(RM)**

delusion: a false, irrational belief arising out of unconscious emotional needs and maintained in spite of logical certainty or proof to the contrary. **(EHB)**

dissociation: separation of normally related mental processes, resulting in one group functioning independently from the rest, leading in extreme cases to disorders such as multiple personality. (**OAD**)

dream: in Jungian dream theory, a vision-like experience that occurs during sleep with images, cognitions, body sensations, and/or emotions, generally in a narrative form, arising from six possible sources: somatic, physical events in the immediate environment, psychical processes perceived by the unconscious, scenes and impressions from earlier life, past events, and future psychical contents. (**RM**)

illusion: a perception of reality not in accord with a more trustworthy perception. (**EHB**)

materialism: a philosophy, worldview, or attitude that only physical matter is real, and everything—including the working of the mind—can be, or will be, explained by a study of physical objects and their interactions. (**RM**)

mental health: a state of well-being in which every individual realizes his or her own potential, can cope with the normal stresses of life, can work productively and fruitfully, and is able to contribute to her or his community. (**WHO**)

panentheism: a view of reality in which that which is infinite pervades the finite but exceeds it; in philosophical and theological terms, God pervades the world but also transcends it. **(RM)**

pantheism: a view that the infinite pervades the finite but does not exceed it; in philosophical and theological terms, God is seen as pervading the universe, "found within nature." **(RM)**

parapsychology: the study of psychological phenomena that are not explained by present-day science. **(RM)**

psyche: a Greek word for soul, sometimes translated also as spirit or mind, but referring in Jungian psychology to the depth dimension of human existence and the reality of life that transcends the body and material existence. **(RM)**

psychoid: a characteristic of the archetype that describes a connection between the material world and psyche. **(RM)**

psychological typology: conceptualized by Carl Jung to account for differences in human personality based upon variations in perception (sensing or intuition) and judging (thinking or feeling). **(RM)**

religion: in its psychological sense, "a state of being grasped by an ultimate concern" (Paul Tillich), or a "... set of symbolic thought forms and acts that relate human beings to the ultimate conditions of existence perceived as the Holy" (W. W. Dever); but in its institutional form, an organization that includes most of the following elements: a cosmology, a sacred text, a moral code, rituals for communal and personal life, devotion to a God-image or iconic figure, and care for suffering. **(RM)**

shadow: behaviors that remain hidden in the human personality and not admitted into consciousness of oneself. **(RM)**

skepticism: an attitude, based upon unconscious needs, of uncertainty or doubt regarding some specific question of fact; or a more pervasive trait of character that appears as a habitual mode of disagreeing, failing to commit, distrusting, and refusing to consider evidence even when it would be in one's self-interest. **(RM)**

symbol: an image that represents an object, behavior, character, or sacred/venerated experience, conveying meaning which cannot be fully explained; unlike a sign, such as a traffic red light in which the image has no further meaning than signaling a stop. **(RM)**

synchronicity: the occurrence of a meaningful coincidence that cannot be explained by the physical laws of cause and effect; also, the field in which the psychoid nature of the archetype brings together the interaction of space, time, mind/psyche, and matter. **(RM)**

theism: belief in the existence of a god or gods, especially belief in a personal God as creator and ruler of the world. **(AHD)**

unconscious: used as an adjective to connote being unaware, but also as a noun in Jungian psychology to describe that part of the psyche from which the conscious arises; described in Jungian psychology as the personal unconscious or the collective unconscious that consists of archetypes and complexes. **(RM)**

NOTES AND REFERENCES

Where I have referenced particular persons or media sources, I note the source in parenthesis, giving the author's name and the date of the work cited. Interested readers may consult the following references to find the full credits.

Regarding Carl Jung's *Collected Works*, I refer to those materials as *CW*, followed by volume and paragraph number. I occasionally refer to Jung's autobiography, *Memories, Dreams, Reflections*, noted as *MDR*.

Arendt, Hannah. *Eichmann in Jerusalem: A Report on the Banality of Evil.* New York: Penguin Books, 2006.

Bair, Deirdre. *Jung: A Biography.* Boston: Little, Brown and Company, 2003.

The Bhagavad Gita. (Mohini M. Chatterji, Trans.). New York: Causeway Books, 1960.

De Waal, F. B. M. *Mama's Last Hug.* New York: W. W. Norton & Co., 2019.

Eliot, T. S. *The Complete Poems and Plays.* New York: Harcourt, Brace and World, Inc. 1971.

Frost, Robert. *A Collection of Poems*. London: Forgotten Books, 2015.

Gamow, George. *Thirty Years that Shook Physics: The Story of Quantum Theory*. New York: Doubleday and Co. Inc., 1966.

Hyams, Joe. *Zen in the Martial Arts*. New York: Jeremy P. Tarcher/Putnam, 1979.

The I Ching or Book of Changes. (R. Wilhelm and C. F. Baynes, Trans.). Bollingen Series XIX, 3d Edition. Princeton: Princeton University Press, 1977.

In the Buddha's Words: An Anthology of Discourses from the Pali Canon. (B. Bodhi, Ed.). Somerville, MA: Wisdom Publications, 2005.

Jung, C. G. *The Collected Works (CW)*. (H. Reed, M. Fordham, G. Adler, Eds.; R. F. C. Hull, Trans.). Princeton, N.J.: Princeton University Press, 1967–78.

_____. *Modern Man in Search of a Soul*. (E. F. Baynes, Ed.; W. S. Dell, Trans.). New York: Houghton Mifflin Harcourt, 1933.

_____. *Memories, Dreams, Reflections.* (A. Jaffe, Ed. and Recorder; R. and C. Winston, Trans.). New York: Random House, Inc., 1963.

Milgram, Stanley. *Obedience to Authority.* New York: Harper and Row, 1974.

The New Jerusalem Bible. New York: Doubleday, 1985.

Pascal, Blaise. *The Thoughts of Blaise Pascal, translated from the text of M. Anguste, Molinier.* (C. K. Paul, Trans.) Wilmington, DE: Veritatis Splendor Publications, 2012.

Sanford, John. *Mystical Christianity.* New York: Crossroad, 1997.

Steinbeck, John. *The Grapes of Wrath.* New York: The Penguin Group, 1976.

Stevens, Anthony. *Archetype Revisited: An Updated Natural History of the Self.* Toronto: Inner City Books, 2003.

Stoner, B. (Executive Producer). (1999). Stoner Productions, Inc. Treasures of the World/bombing of Guernica, www.pbs.org.

The Royal College of Psychiatrists. "Spirituality and Mental Health." www.rcpsych.ac.uk.

Tillich, Paul. *The Meaning of Health: Essays in Existentialism, Psychoanalysis, and Religion.* (P. LeFebre, Ed.) Chicago: Exploration Press, 1984.

Walker, Williston. *A History of the Christian Church.* New York: Charles Scribner's Sons, 1959.

The Way of Life: A New Translation of the Tao Te Ching. (R. B. Blakney, Trans.). New York: New American Library, 1955.

Yeats, William Butler. *Selected Poems and Two Plays of William Butler Yeats.* (M. L. Rosenthal, Ed.) New York: The Macmillan Company, 1962.

PERMISSIONS

INDEX

ABOUT THE AUTHOR

Randall Mishoe maintains a private practice as Jungian Analyst and Pastoral Counselor. His previous work experiences include artillery officer in the US Army with a tour of duty in South Korea, campus minister, and local church pastor. He holds degrees from Clemson University, Southeastern Seminary, Harvard University, and Andover Newton Theological School as well as a Diploma from the C. G. Jung Institute in New England. Among other professional affiliations, Dr. Mishoe is a member of the International Association of Analytical Psychology, and the Association for Clinical Pastoral Education.

Made in the USA
Las Vegas, NV
22 October 2021